Oral Production Rule Book
For Teachers and Learners of North American English

Glenda Reece

ESL Training Services
Raleigh, NC USA
eslts.com

Materials to compile this handout have come from many sources. All efforts have been made to give credit to books and authors within the pages and in the bibliography. However knowledge and information simply becomes a part of a teacher with no intended decision to claim the techniques as one's own. No plagiarism or claim was or is intended. The author truly appreciate the work of Judy Gilbert, Don Snow, Donna Brinton, Carolyn Graham and others in the field. They have truly influenced the author who has adapted and consistently use their insights.

ISBN-10 0-9842813-5-5
ISBN-13 978-0-9842813-5-0

CONTENTS

PRACTICE SESSIONS

Practice sessions are contained in the Table of Contents, but as a convenience are repeated here in a separate list.

ACKNOWLEDGMENTS

Special thanks to my friend and willing editor, Cecelia Barker. Also a big Thank You to William Reece who read and suggested alternatives along the way. This book would not have been possible without the extensive advice, technical help and patience from Preston Reece, my lifelong love and husband.

INTRODUCTION

Purpose

Glenda Reece has spent most of her professional life — more than 40 years — finding and developing the best and most effective methods of teaching everyday spoken English to internationals. This book is the the result of her work. It covers all aspects of learning to speak and listen to casual English. The goal of the book is to help internationals be able to have normal conversations with Americans, and to get jobs and promotions without being limited by their speaking abilities.

Learning a language is more than just building a vocabulary. Many internationals have studied North American English (NAE) in their own country and learned to read and write in English, but they are unable to have a conversation with an American. This may make it difficult to get a job, keep a job or get job promotions.

Spoken English is different from written English. In addition to vocabulary, internationals need to learn the difference between content and structure words, proper use of volume, tone, rhythm, linking of words, sound units, blends and glides. This book explains and provides rules that will help learners speak the way Americans speak.

Learning good oral English is like building a house. Single sounds like vowels, consonants, and syllables along with a small vocabulary form the foundation. They are the first things taught to beginner level students. Sometimes, due to time constraints, they may be the only things taught.

To move forward toward intermediate and advanced levels of English, content words, sound units, structure words and linking rules are added like the walls and a roof are added to the foundation of a house.

To reach fluency, finishing touches such as focal words, rate of speaking, volume control and stress are like the doors, windows, electricity and plumbing of the house. Body language, facial expressions, stamina. voice quality, clarity and intelligibility are important touches to complete the job.

Moving through the steps from beginner to fluency can take years, but learning the rules of the language—many of which are unwritten— will make the job easier.

Three Major Varieties of English

This book offers help with spoken or conversational North American English. For many people reading and writing English are not problems, but clarity in speaking is. It often seems that North American English listeners are impatient and simply will not take the time to listen to slow, poorly spoken English.

British English, Australian English, and North American English, are the three major varieties of the English language spoken in the Great Britain, Australia, and USA. Many other countries use English as their academic or diplomatic languages, but speak their own language at home. India, Nigeria, and other countries throughout the world voted for English to be one of their official languages.

Speakers from countries where English is one of the official languages probably feel they know and use the language correctly. However in English speaking countries other than their own, co-workers still may have difficulty understanding them. They also may feel left out of team interactions, and may not get job promotions as quickly as their associates.

It is frustrating to be passed over in the marketplace because one's English is too overlaid with the sounds and rhythm of their native language. Their English simply is not good enough for them to communicate well. Single sounds can be mispronounced or the speed, rhythm or other property may be wrong and the listener may have to strain or guess what is being said. Many internationals are held back and cannot progress in their chosen profession or job.

Diagnostic Tools

Use the rules and other materials in this book to understand and practice producing correct spoken English. The book gives you tools to diagnose and improve your English. Although most languages have nonverbal components such as speed, rhythm, facial expressions and body language, the expression of those components usually differ from one language to another so even these components must be relearned in order to communicate effectively.

What the Book Contains

This book contains rules, tools, and practice sessions to help teachers, students and self-learners develop a speaking sound and manner similar to North American native speakers.

As a learner who wants to grow in the new language, it may have been difficult to find a teacher or guide who can help you to get better and more relaxed in speaking. This book is a guide to help teachers, students and self-learners to understand the rules and to practice correct spoken English.

Audience

This book is for teachers, students and self-learners of North American English. While self-learners can use the book without a teacher, an assistant who speaks North American English is useful to act as a source to be copied, and as a listener who can judge whether words have been spoken the same way that a native speaker would say them. If a learner simply wants to hear a word, most online dictionaries have a "speaker" icon that one can click to generate the spoken word.

Typographic Conventions

Two forward slashes enclosing one or more letters represent a sound
Example: /s/ for the "sss" sound of an "s"

When the text needs to express a sound of a letter, the letter is enclosed between two forward slashes. For example /s/ represents the *sound* of an "s" when spoken as part of a word, Sometimes there may be more than one letter such as /sh/ to represent the sound that is made when those two letters are spoken together.

A single forward slash inserted in a sentence indicates a sound unit break
Example: Now is the time / for all good men / to come to the aid of their country.

North American English is spoken in short phrases with brief pauses between them. This allows listeners to better understand the speaker, and it gives the speaker an opportunity to take a quick breath if needed. Of course pauses are also inserted at pronunciation marks like commas, semicolons, and periods.

A sound unit break is placed in a logical place as determined by the speaker, and different speakers may choose different places for the break. All words in a sound unit are totally or partially linked.

Y Glides and W Glides

Example: "see us" is pronounced like "seeyus" and may be shown as "see ʸus."

In respellings and in some practice sessions, a "y" or a "w" superscript is sometimes inserted to indicate a y glide or a w glide. This is done to assist in pronunciation. For Down Arrow ↘

A down arrow ↘ is a reminder that one lowers the tone of voice at the end of every sound unit and the end of every sentence. Actually very few sentences or questions in go up in North American English. ↘

Word Thermometer

When a picture of a thermometer is used next to a list of words, it implies that the words have similar meanings, but the words near the top are more specific or more severe depending on the type of list presented.

Words in a Bold Font

In *many of the practice sessions*, **content words** are presented in a **bold** font.

Content words are all question words (such as what, which, when, where, who, whom, whose, why, whether and how *when used in a question,*) nouns, main verbs, adjectives and adverbs. The remaining words are called structure words.

Examples: A **wise old owl sat** in an **oak**
                   A **mouse** in a **house looks** for **cheese** to **eat**
                   Children like to **read books**

Words That Are Underlined

Example: I am so glad that <u>you</u> came to the party.

In *many of the practice sessions*, focal words are <u>underlined</u> to show emphasis.

Focal words are words that a speaker chooses to emphasize. Almost any word in a sentence can be a focal word, but the meaning of the sentence may change based on which word is selected. Do not make every word in a sentence a focal word.

Words That Are Bold and Underlined.

A word that is both bold and underlined indicates a content word that is being used as a focal word.

Words Enclosed in Square Brackets [...]

Square brackets are used to enclose respellings of a word to clarify the sounds that make up a word. Respellings may also separate the syllables in multisyllable words.

Example: Fortune [FOR chu<u>n</u>]

The Most Important Things for Teachers

Provide a safe environment.

Never embarrass a student.

Be prepared with flexible plans.

Ask the student what he or she needs.

Be willing and prepared to explain words or phrases that are uncomfortable for you.

Work to make your students sound like you, and tell them, "Sound like me."

Do not use baby talk or words spoken too slowly. If you need to break long words into syllables, do so and then speak them normally as well. From the very beginning, teach normal English speaking, using normal speed, volume and rhythm.

Remember that spoken words are only a small part of communication. Body language, facial expressions, rhythm and tone are part of the language.

Students learn by doing. *They should do most of the talking.*

Do not over-correct. Keep a focus on the overall purpose of a lesson, and do not give up that objective by spending all of the time correcting simple mistakes that can be dealt with over time.

At the end of each lesson, ask the student "Have you learned anything?" This helps the student to think back and realize what was learned. This is positive reinforcement and helps the student to realize that progress is being made.

The Most Important Things for Students

Do the work.

Practice regularly and often.

Speak and listen to native speakers.

Talk even when it is scary or difficult.

Look at the eyes of the person to whom you are speaking.

It's OK to make mistakes.

It's OK to ask questions.

Learn to sound like your teacher.

Review and read the material aloud many times.

Try making the body language, even though it seems silly.

Mirror the facial expressions of the native speakers when you can.

Goals

Develop Clarity and understandability.

Speak clear and strong consonants and vowels.

Increase Stamina in speaking.

Develop an English voice.

Speak using sound units.

Link the words within a sound unit.

Use focal words.

Use appropriate volume.

Use appropriate tone.

Speak with Power English.

Hear and understand spoken conversational English.

Use appropriate body language.

GETTING STARTED

The Most Important Tool: Repetition

Nothing can replace speaking a word or phrase over and over until it sinks into your long term memory. Teachers will not want to force students to do this, and the students will not want to do it, but it is the *essential* ingredient in learning to speak a language. Very simple words may only require around twenty repetitions, but most words take at least forty or more to move the word into long term memory. The most difficult words can take one hundred or more repetitions.

Only a few new words can be learned in a single lessons, and words learned in a lessons must be reviewed in multiple future lessons.

On the next page is a *Practice Session* to help you remember the importance of repetition. Whenever there is a practice session in the book, the student or self-learner should read it out loud. Preferably, one should do each practice session multiple times. Remember that the words in **bold** are *content words*; however, it does not mean they should be stressed or spoken louder.

Practice: You Need to Say It Many Times

Just because you **say** it **once**
    Doesn't **mean** you **know** it.

You **need** to **say** it **many times**
    Before you really **know** it.

Say it. **Read** it, **Hear** it. **Write** it.
    Say it **again**, **again** and **again**.

Say it. **Read** it. **Hear** it. **Write** it.
    You **need** to **say** it **many times**,
    Many, **many**, **many times**,

Over, and **over** and **over again**.
    Repeat it. **Repeat** it. **Repeat** it. **Repeat** it.

You **need** to **say** it many **times**,
    Many, **many**, **many times**,

Over, and **over** and **over again**.
    Repeat it. **Repeat** it. **Repeat** it. **Repeat** it.

Just because you **say** it **once**
    Doesn't mean you **know** it.

You **need** to **say** it **many times**
    Before you really **know** it.

Just because you **say** it **once**
    Doesn't mean you **know** it.

You **need** to **say** it many **times**
    Before you **really know** it.

—Anonymous. Thanks Phyllis Merritt, for sending it

The Rule of Five

To learn to speak a new word, one must hear it, and speak it out loud many times. This repetition, along with some physical activity, helps to move the word from short term memory to long term memory. The *Rule of Five* provides at least twenty repetitions – the minimum requirement.

1. The teacher speaks the word *five times* while the student listens.

2. The teacher and the student speak the word together *five times*.

3. The student speaks the word *five times* alone while physically counting one to five by touching, in turn, each finger/thumb on one hand with a finger from the other hand. This physical activity helps one to remember the word. While the student speaks, the teacher listens to find areas that need correction.

4. The teacher explains any problems to the student, and the student makes corrections and speaks the word another five times while counting on the fingers as before.

5. Repeat step four *at least* two more times. If problems still exist, step four can be repeated over and over, and steps one and two can be repeated if needed.

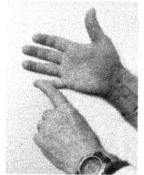

TEACHING STRATEGIES

Bottom-Up Techniques

These include working with single sounds, blends and syllables; learning some tricks; and working with rules. However this is the foundational task and alone it will not bring the speaker toward speaking fluency.

Even low beginners need to combine top-down from the start — including the normal speed and rhythm of sound units and sentences. In the long run, using only bottom-up techniques, the beginner has a really hard time moving from the lowest level of learning. Using top-down techniques a majority of the time in sentences, and then paragraphs, the beginner can quickly improve speaking and English usage skill.

Top-Down Techniques

This includes working with the whole sentence structure with attention to sound units; and working for clarity or accent correction. Using a paragraph or the entire story helps to improve clarity and to build stamina. It enhances the speed of learning and makes even the beginner sentences sound natural. In this book, top-down is emphasized in all cases. Catching single sound discrepancies can be quickly noted and adjusted, and learning continues.

Combine Bottom-Up and Top-Down

Although building a foundation is required, it is important to begin combining top down with bottom up methods as soon as possible. Since this book is not designed for zero level beginners, it will use this combined method from the beginning. Tongue twisters are an effective method to do this and they are fun.

Tongue Twisters Examples

Tongue Twisters are both a challenge and a joy. What can a learner get from practicing them?

Using tongue twisters helps improve clarity in speaking, and provides a fun way to learn the sounds of the language. Learners of all levels grow their speaking skills by practicing both bottom-up and top-down techniques. Furthermore, short sentences repeated together many times increase the stamina of the speaker.

Practice: Whether the Weather
A Tongue Twister for /w/ and /wh/ sounds

Read this out loud several times. It shows minimal pair contrast between the /w/ and /wh/ sounds.

>Whether the weather be fine
>>or whether the weather be not.

>Whether the weather be cold
>>or whether the weather be hot.

>We'll weather the weather
>>whether we like it or not.

Vocabulary

1. **Whether**: A conjunction expressing a doubt or choice

2. **Weather** (as a noun): Cold, hot, wet conditions

3. **Weather** (as a verb): Come safely through a storm. In a broader context, "to weather" means to endure something bad or difficult and be OK.

Exercise: Hold your hand in front of your mouth, and say *whether*. You should feel the air blow against your hand. With the /wh/ sound, the air comes straight out the front of the mouth. Now, hand still in place, say *weather*. Without the /wh/ sound, most of the air goes out the sides of the mouth, and very little comes out the front.

The /th/ sound in "weather" is "voiced." You can feel this by placing your hand on your throat and speaking the word. You will feel your vocal cords vibrate.

Practice: Peter Piper

A Tongue Twister for the /p/ sound

Forward slashes (/) have been added to this tongue twister to mark *sound unit breaks*. Take a slight pause or a "nano breath" at the sound unit marks and at punctuation marks like commas, periods and question marks.

Read the following tongue twister out loud several times.

Peter Piper picked / a peck of pickled peppers.

If Peter Piper picked / a peck of pickled peppers,
how many peppers / did Peter Piper pick?

Peter Piper picked / a peck of pickled peppers,

if Peter Piper picked / a peck of pickled peppers,
where's the peck of pickled peppers /
Peter Piper picked?

Bushel and Peck

Practice the following consonant blends: the /p/ sound when followed by the vowels "e" or "i."

/pee/	as in "Peter"	The long e sound
/peh/	as in "Peck"	The short e sound
/pie/	as in "Piper"	The long i sound
/pi/	as in "Picked"	The short i sound

Continue practicing until you can make all the words link together. "Peter Piper picked / a peck of pickled peppers."

You need to hear the sound of words so that you can mimic them. If there is no teacher or other American English speaker available, you can use an online dictionary. Most online dictionaries can speak words as well as define them. While this is not a perfect solution, it does provide an alternate way when there is no American English speaker available.

Practice: A Fisher Named Fischer
A Tongue Twister for /sh/ sound

The /sh/ sound is a consonant blend. it is often difficult to speak, and the sound /s/ or /ch/ is sometimes incorrectly substituted.

Repeat the following many times - it is a fun challenge.

> There was a young fisher named Fischer
>> Who frequently fished in a fissure.
>
> The fish with a grin,
>> Pulled the fisherman in;
>
> Now they're fishing the fissure
>> for Fischer.

Vocabulary

1. **Fissure** - a long, narrow opening or line of breakage made by cracking or splitting, especially in rock or earth.

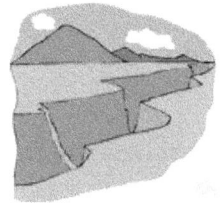

Repeat the following sentence many times. It's a fun challenge:

"The flood was blamed on an unreported fissure in the dam."

Fissure

Vocabulary Expansion: Other Words for Fissure

Opening,	[op/ə/niNG]	Crevice,	[kreh viss]
Crack,	[krak]	Cleft,	[kleft]
Breach,	[breech]	Chasm;	[ka zm]
Break,	[breik] [brak]	Fracture,	[frak chr]
Fault,	[faalt]	Rift,	[Rift]
Rupture,	[Ruhp chr]	Split.	[Split]

Speaking and Communicating includes learning many new words. Using them in context really helps.

Practice: Greek Grape Growers

A Tongue Twister for the /gr/ consonant blend sound

The great Greek grape growers /
grow great Greek grapes.

Working on consonant blends: /gr/ sound

Remember, for vowels, the long sound always sounds just like the name of the character: A, E, I, O, U.

Note: to indicate that a character should be pronounced with a long sound, the character may be displayed as the character with a bar over it like ā.

The long sound of /ā/ or /aye/ as in great. (The e in "great" is silent.)
The long sound of /ē/ as in Greek.
The long sound of /ā/ as in Grape.
The long sound of /ō/ as in growers and grow.

Strong consonants ending a word:

The sound /t/ in great
The sound /p/ in grape
The sound /k/ in Greek.

Linking "Stop" Sounds

The sound /k/ and /g/ in Gree<u>k g</u>rapes are both "stop" sounds (once you voice them, you cannot continue the sound. (Unlike the /s/ sound which is not a stop sound and can go on as long as you want, like /sssssss/.)

To *link* the two words, the /k/ sound in "Greek" is placed in the mouth, but gets no air ("gree^k"); The /k/ sound is not omitted, but the air goes to the /g/ sound in "grapes".

Do not insert an /uh/ filler sound between the /k/ at the end of Greek and the /g/ at the beginning of grapes. *Do not say "GREE kuh GRAPES ."*

Syllables

"The basic unit of English rhythm is the syllable," by Judy Gilbert, *Clear Speech*.

Counting syllables while performing a physical action helps the brain to learn to speak all of the syllables in a words.

One way to count the syllables is to count on your fingers - one finger for each syllable. Or you can clap your hands or snap your fingers as you say each syllable.

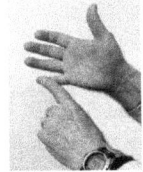

You can also use these methods to count words in a sound unit or sentence.

Blends and Syllables

Syllables *(note: syllables that are emphasized are in CAPITAL letters)*

One Syllable	Two Syllables	Three Syllables
John [Jahn]	Preston	Gwendolyn [GWEN duh lynn]
Joy	Joyful	Joyfully [JOY fuh lee]
Add	Compute	Computer [com PU der]

Four Syllable	Five Syllables	Six Syllables
Technology [Teck KNAH luh gee]	Technological [Tek no LODG uh kal]	Humanitarian [Hugh man uh TAR re un]
Incredible [In CRED uh bul]	Customizable [kus tuh MIZ uh bul]	Disciplinarian [Dis suh plin NAR re un]
Psychologist [Sigh KAH luh gist]	Vocabulary [Vo CAB you lar ree]	Parliamentarian [Par luh men TAR re un]
Community [Ka MUN nuh tee]	I want a large COKE	I want a large SAND wich

Respelling is one of the methods that help learners pronounce words using North American English sounds. Teachers have different opinions on this, but generally, learners like it, and find it useful. However, always use the *correct* spelling in your writing.

Practice: The Goose That Laid the Golden Egg

This exercise uses a bold font for content words and includes *sound unit marks* All the words in a sound unit should be linked together. The sound unit, "/*and his wife/*," sounds like "/*andiswife/*." *Wife* is a content word and must be said clearly.

A **Man** / and his **Wife** / had the **good fortune** / to **possess** a **Goose** / which **laid** a **Golden Egg every day.** / **Lucky** though they were, / they **soon began to think** / they were **not getting rich fast enough**, / and, / **imagining** the **bird** <u>**must**</u> be **made** of **gold inside,** / they **decided** to **kill** it / in **order** to **secure** / the **whole store** of **precious metal** / at **once.** / **But** / when they **cut** it **open** / they **found** it was <u>**just**</u> like **any other goose.** / Thus, / they <u>**neither**</u> **got rich all** at **once,** / as they had **hoped**, / <u>**nor**</u> **enjoyed any longer** / the **daily addition** to their **wealth.**

Moral: "**Much**" **wants more** and **loses all.**

Syllables *(note: syllables that are emphasized are in CAPITAL letters)*

One Syllable	Two Syllables [with respelling]	Three Syllables [with respelling]
Man	Fortune [FOR chu<u>n</u>]	Imagining [uh MAJ juh ning]
Wife	Possess [po ZESS]	Decided [Dee SIDE ded]
Goose	Golden [GOL dun]	Addition [Uh DISH shun]
Wealth [Welth]	Lucky [LUH key.]	
Hoped [Hōwpt]	Getting [GED ding]	
	Precious [PRAY shu<u>s</u>]	
	Enjoyed [in JOID]	
	Loses [LOO zez]	*(Respelling with help from Google.)*

Blends

Blends occur when two or three consonants are pronounced together. In the word, *blend,* the consonants *b* and *l* and *n* and *d* form the word with the vowel *e.* Pronunciation of the word blend, a one syllable word, requires no extra sounds. In *The Goose That Laid The Golden Egg*, there are several blends: *golden, gold, longer* and *wealth.*

BOTTOM-UP: THE BRICKS AND BLOCKS OF ENGLISH

Vowels

Vowels are the core or peak of a syllable. They are single sounds with a continual vibration (continuants) of the vocal chords and the air stream escapes from the mouth unobstructed. It is difficult to "place" vowels in the mouth.

English has only five vowels (a, e, i, o, u) but all vowels have more than one sound depending on blends and adjacent consonants. Many of the vowel sounds in American English are similar to sounds in other languages; however some sounds are unique to American English. Those learning the language must hear and speak the new sounds.

Speaking some new sounds will require using muscles in the mouth and throat that have not been used before, and may also require different breath control.

Vowel Chart with IPA Symbols

The IPA (International Phonetic Alphabet) symbols are beside the key words.

Vowel Chart								
The chart contains some IPA symbols for the sounds and key words.								
Long Vowel Sounds (they sound like their name)			**Short Vowel Sounds**			**Difficult Vowel Sounds**		
a	/e/	face	a	/æ/	apple	a	/ɔ:/	ball
e	/i/	key	e	/ɛ/	egg		/a/	car
i	/ay/	mice	i	/I/	in	i	/ɚ/	bird
o	/o/	coat	o	/ɒ/	olive	o	/u:/	moon
u	/u/	music	u	/ʌ/	up, cup		/ʊ/	book
The schwa (ə) can replace any vowel in an unstressed position							/aʊ/	cow
							/ɔɪ/	boy

A Schwa Is a Reduced or *Unstressed* Vowel

The most used single sound in English is the schwa, which is the sound of a reduced or unstressed vowel. Many English language learners are unaware of it, and therefore are frequently misunderstood; or are self-conscious about their speech but don't realize it's because the *unstressed* schwa sound is missing. It can sound like /uh/, so that is a common respelling used in this guide.

The symbol for a Schwa is "ə" which looks like an upside down "e" and has an *unstressed* /uh/ sound as in the word "variety" which would be shown as "vəriəty."

A short list of common words that show the use of the schwa /ə/ and one example of a carat, /ʌ/, which is for a stressed "u" sound as in the word "up."

Corporation [Cor pə ra tion]	Preparation [Prep ə ra tion]	Variety [V ə ri ə ty]	Compete [Cəm pete]
Especially [ə spe shə lly]	Symptoms [Symp təms]	Problem [Prah bləm]	Tendency [Ten dən see]
Prominent [Prah mə nənt]	Little [Lit əl]	Capsul [Cap səl]	Security [Sə cur rə ty]
Habitually [Hə bi chew əl ly]	Adequate [Adə kwəte]	Feminine [Fem ə nəne]	Abolish [ə bah lish]
Ribbon [Rib bən]	Document [Docu mənt]	Maryland [Marə lənd]	Ultimate [Ul tə mə te]
Salaries [Sal ə reeez]	Undeniable [Un de ni ə ble]	Funding /ʌ/ Stressed [Fʌn ding] (Use /ə/ only for *unstressed*)	

R-Colored, L-Colored, and N-Colored Vowels

What are r-colored, l-colored, and n-colored vowels? Vowels are affected or "colored" when certain consonants follow them.

Practice: Colored Vowels

Using a rubber band, read the pairs aloud. Listen for the differences in the way the vowel sound actually changes or colors slightly. Using the rubber band is a way to add physical movement that enforces the speaking and helps one to learn better. (see below for how to use the rubber band.)

Vowels: R, L or N colored				
bead	beard		hep	help
fed	fared		boy	boil
hut	hurt		my	mile
see	seal		how	hound

How to use a rubber band in this practice

place a rubber band on the thumbs of both hands and hold your hands in front of your chest. As you speak the content word(s), stretch the rubber band by separating your hands quickly. After speaking the word(s), move your hands close together again, and go to the next content word(s).

Note: a size 64 rubber band (1/4 inch wide) works best. It is less likely to break than thinner ones.

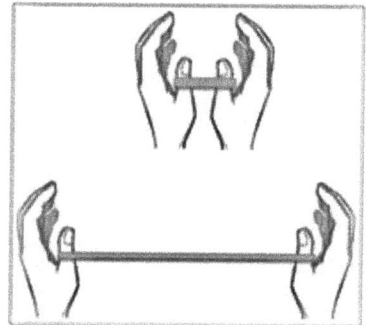

Practice: Tomoko the Journalist

/ɚ/, /er/ and /ur/ Sound Vowel as In H**er**, W**or**k, Jo**ur**nal

This exercise uses a bold font for content words and includes *sound unit marks.* All the words in a sound unit should be linked together.

Tomoko wanted to **become** a **journalist.** / Her **purpose** was to **cover** the **worthy news stories** / **all** over the **world.** / She **understood** the **power** of the **written word,** / and **her first stories earned** her **worldwide attention.** / She **went** / **wherever** her **work took** her / and **always wanted** to be the **earliest reporter** / to **get** the **stories out** on the **wire services.** / **People** were **surprised** / when they **met this tiny Japanese woman.** / Her **greatest series** of **stories** / **won** her an **American Pulitzer Prize.** / She **wrote honestly** / about **tensions** in the **competing business world** / of **American** and **Japanese workers.** / She **felt** her **contribution** / was to **report worthy stories** / and **discount worthless rumors.** / She **disliked writing** about **murder** and **violent crimes,** / but **really liked** to **cover** the **business stories.** / She **earned respect** / in the **world of news** and **travel.** / This **reporter** was **really worth** her **salt.**

Practice: /ɝ/, /ur/, and /er/ Sounds

These words have the /er/ sound or the /ur/ sound. All of the practice words are from the previous story. This sound is used only in North American English.

Note: The phonetic symbol for this sound looks similar to a schwa, but has a tiny "r" attached on the right side /ɚ/ . Use your online dictionary to hear the sounds, and learn which muscles, or articulators to use (for example: lips, tongue, soft and hard palate.)

Be sure to say the entire word including the ending. For example, don't say *were* or *word* for *world. Be sure to get in the "l" and the "d."* [<u>WUR</u> ul d]

/ɚ/, /er/, and /ur/ sounds			
Her [hur]	**Journalist** [Jur nuh luhst]	**Purpose** [Pur puhs]	**Services** [Sur vuh sez]
Worthy [wur thee]	**Worthless** [Wurth lessl	**Wherever** [weh reh vr]	**Power** [Po^w ɚ] or [pow ur]
Word [wurd]	**First** [furst]	**Earned** [urnd]	**World** [Wur ul d] or [wurld]
Work [wurk]	**Earliest** [ur lee uhst]	**Wire** [wai ur]	**Reporter.** [Ruh por dɚ]
Cover [kuh ver]	**Surprised** [sur prizd]	**Workers** [wurkerz]	**Pulitzer.** [pew lit zer]

"Worth her salt" is an Idiom that means the person is competent at the job they are doing, and deserving of the pay they receive. It comes from Ancient Rome where soldiers were sometimes paid in salt.

Consonants

Consonants – all the letters that are not vowels - make up the solid blocks on which we construct words, phrases and sentences. The blocks are connected by the fluid vowels.

Consonant Chart with IPA Symbols

Consonant Chart			
The chart contains some IPA symbols for the sounds and key words.			
Consonant Pairs Unvoiced and Voiced		Other Consonant Sounds Voiced	
/p/ pan	/b/ bird	**Nasals:**	**Other Sounds:**
/t/ tent	/d/ dish	/m/ man	/h/ hand
/k/ kick	/g/ girl	/n/ neck	/ks/ bo<u>x</u>
/ch/ children	/ʤ/ jump	/ŋ/ ri<u>ng</u>	/l/ leg
/f/ fish	/v/ valley		/kw/ quarter
/s/ snake	/z/ zipper	**Glottal stop:**	/r/ road
/ʃ/ shop	/ʤ/ mea<u>sure</u>	/ʔ/ bo*tt*le,	/y/ yell
/θ/ thank	/ð/ this		
/hw/ /⟨ʍ⟩/ whistle	/w/ wing		

Voiceless *th* Sound

Place the tip of the tongue on the back of the two upper front teeth, near the bottom, then blow gently. The air will flow around the tongue and out the sides of the mouth.

Beginning	Medial	Ending		Minimal Pairs				
Think	Method	Worth		Think	Sink		Thin	Sin
Thank	Mother	Wealth		Thud	Dud		With	Wit
Thumb	Father	With		Mother	Mutter		Myth	Miss

Practice: *Thread the Needle*, and *I Thought*

Thread the Needle

Use the needle threader /
    To thread the needle.

Think I can thread it?
    Well, I thought so.

I Thought ...

I thought I thought /
    the thought I thought.

Contractions

Contractions
Use a rubber band and your fingers to teach and un-teach these. Contractions are not generally stressed, and can often be very short. They are generally structure words.

Full Form	Contraction		Full Form	Contraction
I am	I'm		he has	he's
is not	isn't		I will	I'll
they have	They've		I have	I've

Task: *Use a rubber band and your fingers to practice these.*

Contractions are not generally stressed, and can often be spoken quickly, and these contractions are only one syllable.

Try using a gross (large muscle) motor movement. For "I am" touch the shoulder and the hand.

For the word or contraction, *I'm,* Touch the tip of a finger and in one smooth movement slide the hand or fingers down the arm to the elbow.

Try "you haven't" and use the entire arm.

Also, counting off on fingers works, too.

Reductions

Reductions are reduced forms of English words strung together, such as "cuddabin" for "could have been." Reductions are not real words; they are several words or sound units spoken casually as a single word, and are a normal way of speaking. English learners need to know reductions in order to understand, or talk like, a native English speaker.

Making Contractions and Reductions	
Formal English	**Fast Casual English with Respelling.**
He should have been home:	He should've been home. He shudduhbin home.
I could have, should have, would have, but I did not.	I could've; should've; would've; but I didn't. I cudda, shudda, wudda, but I didn't.
They had been driving for hours.	They'd bin drivin' for hours.
It would be fun to do.	It'd be fun ta do.

The -tion Rule

If a noun ends in "-tion" or "-sion," the sound before it is held longer that usual. Here are some examples. Occasionally, respelling is used to help in pronunciation.

Nation [NA shun]	Stimulation [Stim u LAY tion]	Relation [Re LAY tion]	Situation [Sit chew WAY shun]
Station [STA shun]	Reparation [Re pa RA tion]	Omission [O MIS shun]	Refrigeration [Ree frig jer RAY shun]
Mission [MISH shun]	Distribution [Dis trə BU shun]	Permission [Per MISH shun]	Registration [Reg əh STRA shun]
Fashion [FASh shun]	Creation [Cre ^{Y}A shun]	Elation [EE LAY shun]	Election [EE LEK shun]

The Flap /d/ Rule

The /t/ sound takes on a unique quality after a vowel, an /r/ sound, or an unstressed syllable. The tongue touches the tooth ridge very briefly, like a flap or a tap, and it is voiced.

This also occurs in the same situations where the /d/ is found. There is little or no sound difference in words like *catty* and *caddy.*

These flaps also occur in sentences and across word boundaries. For example, *Part it on the side. [PARditonthuhSIDE]*

(Note: The Flap /d/ is found only *in North American English)*

Water	Traitor	City	Sitting
Pretty	Ditty	Ladder	Dirty
Waiter	Later	Started	Matter
Data	Cut it out! [Cudidout]	Made it all red [Mayditdall red]	Heat it Heed it (They sound the same)

Past Tense Regular Verbs

Rule: The letter combination *ed* has more than one sound.

It usually has the /t/ sound when *ed* is added to words ending in *f, k, s, sh, ch*, and *x*.

It usually has the /ed/ sound when the base word has the final /t/ or final /d/ sound.

When *ed* is added to words ending in other letter, it usually had the /d/ sound.

/t/ words ending in *f, k, s, sh, ch*, and *x*.	/ed/ words ending in *t* or *d*	/d/ words where *ed* is added, but base word did not end with *t* or *d*
Accessed	Automated	Arrived
Accomplished	Bounded	Called
Asked	Consecrated	Cleaned
Cooked	Created	Compromised
Dressed	Crated	Conceived
Finished	Dated	Earned
Increased	Dedicated	Encircled
Kissed	Distributed	Engaged
Laughed	Exalted	Entered
Liked. Disliked	Graded	Filled
Looked	Handed	Followed
Wished	Regulated	Specialized

Make the *sounds* that *f, k, s, sh, ch*, and *x* represent. Place your hand right at your mouth and you can feel the air quickly exhale. The /t/, /d/, and the /ed/ sounds are the stops. If needed, exaggerate the ending sound until the ending sound can be heard by the listener.

Say: The name of the letter is "F", the sound of the letter is ... (make the sound)

Practice: The Gettysburg Address

Four score and **seven years ago** / our **fathers brought forth**, / upon this **continent**, / a **new nation**, / **conceived** in Liberty, /and **dedicated** / to the **proposition** / that <u>all</u> men / are **created equal.**

Now we are **engaged** in a **great Civil War**, / **testing** whether that **nation**, / or <u>any</u> nation, / **so conceived**, / and **so dedicated**, / can **long endure**. / We are **met here** / on a **great battle-field** / of that **war**. / We have **come** / to **dedicate** a **portion** of it / as a **final resting place** / for those / who <u>here</u> gave their lives /that that **nation** might live. / It is **altogether fitting** / and **proper** / that we should **do** <u>this</u>. /

But / in a **larger sense** / we **cannot dedicate** —/ we **cannot consecrate** —/ we **cannot hallow** this **ground**. / The **brave men**, / **living** and **dead**, / who **struggled here**, / have **consecrated** it / **far above** our **poor power** / to **add or detract**. / The **world** will **little note**, / nor **long remember**, / what <u>we</u> <u>say</u> here, / but can **never forget** / what <u>they did</u> here. / It is for us, / the **living**, / **rather** to be **dedicated here** / to the **unfinished work** / which they **have**, / **thus far**, / **so nobly carried on**. /

It is **rather** for us / to **be here dedicated** / to the **great task** /**remaining** before us —/ that from these **honored dead** / we **take increased devotion** / to that **cause** / for which they <u>here</u> / **gave** the **last full measure** of **devotion** —/ that we **here highly resolve** / that these **dead** shall **not** have **died in vain**; / that this **nation** shall have a **new birth** of **freedom**; / and that this **government** / <u>of</u> the **people**, / <u>by</u> the **people**, / <u>for</u> the **people** / shall **not perish** / from the **earth**. /

/t/	/d/	/ed/
Unfinished	Engaged	Created
Increased	Conceived	Dedicated
	Struggled	Consecrated
	Carried on	
	Honored	

-tion Rule: nation, proposition, portion, and devotion

Two Word Verb: carry on

Flap D Rule: battle-field, fitting, consecrated, little.

Vocabulary

1. **Score:** In old English, score was a set of twenty. This is how Lincoln used it. In the plural form, we could say that *A score of men fought against the wildfires.*

    Today we use score, as in scoring points in a game, a rating or a grade, or in slang, such as buying an illegal drug. Older English words can have many meanings.

2. **To conceive:** To plan or have a good idea for something. It is also used to mean to become pregnant with a child.

3. **To dedicate:** To formally open or unveil a monument to memorial. Also it means to devote time or effort to something.

4. **To consecrate:** To make or declare something sacred. To devote something, like a battlefield to an exclusive purpose.

TOP-DOWN PRONUNCTION

- Sound Units
- Content Words
- Structure Words
- Correct Use of Stress
- Focal Words
- Stamina in Speaking
- Increased Vocabulary and Related Words
- Better Comprehension
- Linking Rules and Usage
- Correct Rate of Speaking
- Rhythm of the language
- Voice Quality for NAE
- Low English Tone
- Volume and Tone
- Speaking with Expression
- Emotions, Feeling and Energy
- Power English
- Clarity and Intelligibility
- Body Language and Facial Expression
- Movement toward Fluency
- Compressions and Reductions

English Is a Stressed Timed Language

— From Rhythm and Unstress, by Howard B. Woods

English typically has a predetermined rhythm, and the syllables seem to scramble to accommodate the beat. The rhythm has a major stressed syllable about every 0.6 seconds, and there maybe one or two unstressed syllables near stressed syllable.

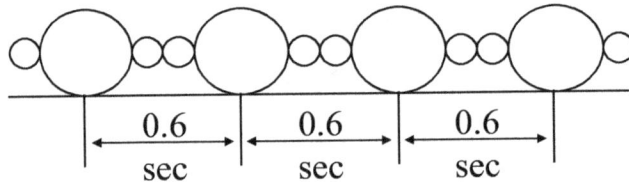

The rhythm of a typical English sentence

The rhythm is maintained by the stressed syllables. If there are several unstressed syllables around the stressed syllable, its duration is shortened, and the unstressed syllables must be glided over very rapidly.

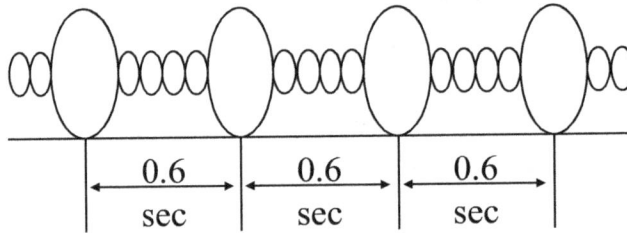

The rhythm of several unstressed syllables

If there are no unstressed syllables nearby, the stressed syllables are naturally lengthened in order to fill the spaces of 0.6 sec intervals.

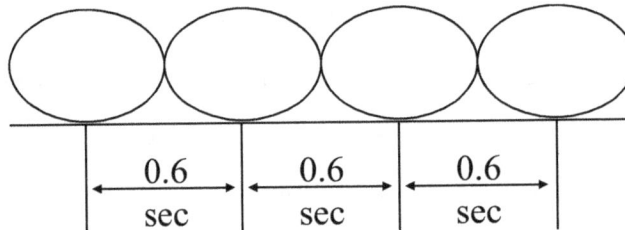

The rhythm of NO unstressed syllables

Look at the following two sentences. They demonstrate the rhythm and stressed timed features of the English language.

The cat is interested in protecting her kittens.

Large cars waste gas.

In the first sentence, a native English speaker will rush over the unstressed syllables (structure words) so as to gain time for the full pronunciation of the stressed syllables; in the second sentence, every word is a stressed syllable and the speaker will stretch them out and produce less linking in order to compensate for the lack of unstressed syllables. *As a result, the duration and the rhythm is the same for both sentences.*

In the "bubble" practice that follow, words in small bubbles are linked and are spoken fast because they are *structure* words; the words in large bubbles are *content* words and take up most of the time. Content words form the rhythm of the sentence.

Practice: The Wise Old Owl

Beginner Level

A wise old owl sat in an oak.

The more he heard the less he spoke.

The less he spoke the more he heard.

Why aren't we all like the wise old bird?

Intermediate to Advanced Level - casual, using compressions and linking

A wyzoldowl sat inanoak.

The mor'e heard the less'e spoke.

The less'e spoke the mor'e heard.

Why arentweeyal like the wyzolbird?

Sound Units

- Basic Spoken English
- Do not speak in single words
- Do not break a natural sound unit
- All sound units are linked to the words within the sound unit
- Stress is length, not volume
- Music helps you hear the sound units

Remember that native speakers talk in sound units. That means that there is no breaking apart of natural units, like prepositional phrases, and short phrases in a series. *A sound unit is one entire phrasal utterance with no breath to break it.* It is frequently linked in sound, and could easily be mistaken for one word. Sometimes sound units are set off by commas, and form natural phrasal patterns. However, in normal speaking, all prepositional phrases are sound units, the verb in all its parts is a sound unit, and generally the entire subject with all the modifiers is a sound unit.

Try to mark the natural sound units. Most of our short sentences are only one sound unit. *Pick up the pencil. Hold that door!* would each be only one sound unit. Longer sentences break into sound units and that is where the learner can pause briefly and take a quick breath if needed, then continue. Many learners mark sounds units according to the way they speak. Examples in this text have the sound units broken with a / slash mark. (/) This does not happen in silent reading, but in speaking the language.

Understanding and Speaking the long sentence

Dividing long sentences / into sound units / really helps with comprehension / and gives a clearer understanding. / The following story has only four sentences. / In the original form, / it is one paragraph.

Practice: The Shepherd's Boy and the Wolf

A **Shepherd's Boy** / was **tending** his **flock** near a **village**, / and **thought** it would be **great fun** / to **hoax** the **villagers** / by **pretending** / that a **Wolf** was **attacking** the **sheep**: / so he **shouted out**, / "**Wolf! Wolf!**" / and when the **people came running up** / he **laughed** at them for their **pains**.

He did this <u>**more**</u> than **once**, / and **every time** the **villagers found** / they had been **hoaxed**, / for there was **no Wolf** at **all**.

At last / a **Wolf** <u>**really**</u> **did come**, / and the **Boy cried**, / "**Wolf! Wolf!**" / as **loud** as he **could**: / but the people / were **so used** to **hearing** him **call** / that they **took** <u>**no**</u> **notice** / of his **cries** for **help**.

<u>And so</u> / the **Wolf** had it **all his own way**, / and **killed off sheep** after **sheep** at his **leisure**.

Moral: You **cannot believe** a **liar** / <u>**even**</u> when he **tells** the **truth**.

Speaking and reading the long sentence

Pause briefly and take a breath if needed at sound unit marks. Within the sound units, speak the words all together without long pauses or additional sounds. The underlined words are focal words, and should be emphasized. Content words are in **bold** and structure words are normal.

Vocabulary

1. **Flock:** A group of sheep or birds.
2. **To hoax:** (verb) To trick or deceive.
3. **A hoax;** (noun) A trick or deception.
4. **Pains:** Great effort. Great care and trouble.
5. **To be used to:** Familiar with. Accustomed to something.

Practice: The Pledge of Allegiance

I Pledge allegiance / to the flag / of the United States / of America /
and to the republic / for which it stands. / One nation / under God / indivisible /
with liberty and justice / for all.

Practice: Eisenhower Statement

Every gun that is made, / every warship launched, /
 every rocket fired /
signifies, / in the final sense, /
 a theft/ from those who hunger/ and are not fed, /
 those who are cold / and are not clothed. /
This world / in arms / is not spending money alone. /

It is spending the sweat of its laborers, /
the genius of its scientists, /
the hopes of its children. /

—President and General Dwight D. Eisenhower

Stress

Stress is length, not volume.
For example: I **don't** want you to **do** that.

Stress the words *don't* and *do* and hold each longer, not necessarily louder.

Leadership Quotes

Lead me, **follow** me, or **get** out of my **way**. —*General George Patton*

What does this tell you about determination or power?

You **manage things**; you **lead people**. —*Rear Admiral Grace Murray Hopper*

Can you name two or three ways a person can lead?

You **don't need** a **title** to be a **leader**. —*Multiple Attributions*

Who do you know is a leader without a title? At work? In your circle of friends?

A **leader** is **one** who **knows** the **way**, **goes** the **way**, and **shows** the **way**.
—*John Maxwell*

In business or in a laboratory, how would this work out?
How does a parent lead his family?

My **own definition** of **leadership** is this: The **capacity** and the **will** to **rally men** and **women** to a **common purpose** and the **character** which **inspires confidence**.

—*General Montgomery*

How can a person find a common purpose with a group or a team at work or in the family?

Practice: I've Learned

- I've **learned** / that you can **tell** a **lot** about a **person** / by the **way** he or she **handles three things:** —a **rainy day** / —**lost luggage,** / and —**tangled Christmas tree lights.**

- I've **learned** that, / **regardless** of your **relationship** with your **parents,** you'll **miss** them / when they're **gone** from your **life.**

- I've **learned** / that **making** a **"living"** / is **not** the **same thing** / as **making** a **"life."**

- I've **learned** / that **life** <u>sometimes</u> **gives** you a **second chance.**

- I've **learned** / that you **shouldn't go** through **life** / with a **catcher's mitt** on **both hands.** / You **need** to be ʸable / to **throw something back.**

- I've **learned** that if you **pursue happiness,** / it will **elude** you. / **But,** / if you **focus** on your **family,** / your **friends,** / the **needs** of **others,** / your **work** and **doing** the **very best** you can, **happiness** <u>will</u> **find** you.

- I've **learned** / that **whenever** I **decide something** / with an **open heart,** / I <u>usually</u> **make** the **right decision.**

- I've **learned** / that <u>even</u> when I have **pains,** / I **don't** have to <u>be</u> one.

- I've **learned** / that **every day,** / you **should reach out** / and **touch** someone. **People love** / that **human touch** / —**holding hands,** / a **warm hug,** / or just a **friendly pat** on the **back.**

- I've **learned** / that I <u>still</u> have a **lot** to **learn.**

- I've **learned** / that you **should pass this on** / to **everyone** you **care about.** / I **just did.** / **Sometimes** / they **just need** a **little something** / to **make them smile.**

People will **forget** what you **said** ... / **people** will **forget** what you **did** ... / but **people** will <u>never</u> **forget** / how you **made** them **feel.**

—Attributed to many people including Carl Buehler & Maya Angelou

Stamina in Speaking

It takes a great deal of brain glucose to speak a second language. The native language takes little or no energy, but the second language is exhausting for the learner. ESL books seldom use many sentences to teach the lesson. Therefore, learners spend years doing short exercises and never learn to tell a story or to read a long passage aloud. Many persons have never spoken the second language for more than two to three minutes at a time. They spend years in this country listening, and watching, but letting others do the explaining.

Practice: The Wooden Bowl

A **frail old man** / **went** to **live** with his **son,** / **daughter-in-law,** / and **four-year old grandson.** / The **old man's hands trembled,** / his **eyesight** was **blurred,** / and his **step faltered.** / The **family ate together** at the **table.** / **But** / the **elderly grandfather's shaky hands** / and **failing sight** / **made eating difficult.** / **Peas rolled off** his **spoon** onto the **floor.** / When he **grasped** the **glass,** / **milk spilled** on the **tablecloth.** / The **son** and **daughter-in-law** / **became irritated** with the **mess.** / We **<u>must do</u> something** about **Grandfather,"** / **said** the **son.** / I've had **<u>enough</u>** of his **spilled milk,** / **noisy eating,** / and **food** on the **floor.** / **So** / the **husband** and **wife** / **set** a **small table** in the **corner.** / **There,** / **Grandfather ate alone** / while the **rest** of the **family** / **enjoyed dinner.**

Since Grandfather had broken a **dish** or **two,** / his **food** was **served** in a **wooden bowl.** / When the **family glanced** in **Grandfather's direction,** / **sometimes** he had a **tear** in his **eye** as he **sat alone.** / **Still,** / the **only words** the **couple had** for him / were **sharp admonitions** / when he **dropped** a **fork** / or **spilled food.**

The **four-year-old watched it all** in **silence.** / **One evening** before **supper,** / the **father noticed** his **son** / **playing** with **wood scraps** on the **floor.** / He **asked** the **child sweetly,** / "**What** are you **making?**"

Just as **sweetly,** / the **boy responded,** / "**Oh,** I am **making** a **little bowl** / for you and **Mama** / to **eat** your **food** / when I **grow up.**" / The **four-year-old smiled** / and **went back** to **work.**

The **words <u>so</u> struck** the **parents** / that they were **speechless.** / **Then** / **tears started** to **stream down their cheeks.** / Though **no word** was **spoken,** / **both knew** / what **must be done.** / **That evening** / the **husband took Grandfather's hand** / and **gently led** him **back** to the **family table.** / For the **remainder** of his **days** / he **ate <u>every</u> meal** with the **family.** / **And** / for some **reason,** / **neither husband nor wife** / **seemed** to **care any longer** / when a **fork** was **dropped,** / **milk spilled,** / or the **tablecloth soiled.**

Children are **remarkably perceptive.** / Their **eyes <u>ever</u> observe,** / their **ears <u>ever</u> listen,** / and **their minds <u>ever</u> process** / the **messages** they **absorb.** / **If** they **see us patiently provide** / a **happy home atmosphere** for **family members,** / they will **imitate** that **attitude** / for the **rest** of their **lives.** / The **wise parent realizes** / that **every day** / the **building blocks** are being **laid** / for the **child's future.** / **Let's be wise builders** and **role models.**

Vocabulary

1. **Frail**: Weak and delicate, for a person. Easily damaged, like a special wine glass.

2. **Trembled**: Shake involuntarily. Being apprehensive or fearful as in *Tremble to think of losing her job.*

3. **Blurred**: Unable to see clearly.

4. **Faltered**: Begin to lose strength or momentum. *He faltered in his speech because he was too emotional to speak more.*

5. **Shaky**: Trembling and likely to drop something.

6. **Grasped**. Seized or held firmly or strongly.

7. **Irritated**. Showing slight anger or irritation.

8. **Mess**: Dirty or untidy state of a place.

9. **Spilled**: Cause liquid to fall over a container.

10. **Sharp** admonitions: loud or strong warning to someone.

11. **Scraps**: Small or left-over pieces of something.

12. **Soiled**: Dirty.

13. **Remarkably perceptive**: Understanding. Clear sensitivity to something.

14. **Tangled**: Twisted untidily. *Her hair was a tangled mess when she woke up.*

15. **Catcher's mitt**: Large and special glove used in a baseball game.

16. **To be a pain**: To make others feel irritated or annoyed. Also known as a pain in the neck (or butt).

Flap/d/ words: Attitude [add uh chewD]; Eating [ē ding]

Linking rules in this story

1. Linking with /y/ or /w/ glides. A fra^{y}il old man; You **need** to be ^{y}able ; **see ^{y}us patiently provide; re^{y}alizes, So^{y}iled; enjoy^{w}ed dinner; does go ^{w}on; The family ^{y}ate;**

2. When a word ending with a single consonant is followed by a vowel. Hold the consonant so it sounds like it belongs to both words. This is very common.

   The frail old man; his **eyesight; milk spilled on**

3. When a word or syllable ending in a consonant cluster is followed by a word beginning with a vowel, the final consonant is pronounced as if it belongs to both words.

   Years earlier, strong and healthy, almost over

4. When a word ends with a consonant and the next word begins with that same consonant sound, the sound is elongated, but is never produced twice and no extra filler sound is used.

   went to live with his son; and his step faltered. rolled off his spoon; he grasped the glass

5. The stops in English are t, d, p, k, g, and j.

   We must do something about Grandfather

6. *T or D plus you or your*

   to eat your food [sounds like *eatcher*]

Pronunciation Practice for Past Tense Regular Verbs

"ed" sounds like /t/	"ed" sounds like /d/		"ed" sounds like /ed/
Grasped	Trembled	Rolled off	Irritated
Glanced	Blurred	Spilled	Responded
Dropped	Faltered	Enjoyed	Started
Watched	Served	Smiled	
Noticed	Seemed	Soiled	
Asked	Learned		

Content Words

When speaking, the content words are emphasized by taking up most of the time and setting the rhythm.

- Question words when used in a question
  (who, what, where, when, why, how)
- Nouns
- Verbs (main verbs only)
- Adjectives
- Adverbs

Content words are in **bold** font

A Time for Everything

Team One	Team Two
A **time** to be **born**	A **time** to **die**
A **time** to **kill**	A **time** to **heal**
A **time** to **tear down**	A **time** to **build**
A **time** to **weep**	A **time** to **laugh**
A **time** to **mourn**	A **time** to **dance**
A **time** to **embrace**	A **time** to **refrain**
A **time** to **search**	A **time** to **give up**
A **time** to **keep**	A **time** to **throw away**
A **time** to **tear down**	A **time** to **mend**
A **time** to be **silent**	A **time** to **speak**
A **time** to **love**	A **time** to **hate**
A **time** for **war**	A **time** for **peace**
There is a **time** for **everything**!	

—Ancient Text: Ecclesiastes 3: 2-8

Structure Words

Structure words are spoken quickly and are unstressed.

- Reduced, unstressed
- Pronouns, prepositions, articles
- Conjunctions and contractions
- In Music, content words would be whole notes, and structure words may be half notes, quarter notes, etc. as needed to fill the gaps and fit the rhythm.
- Structure words are *not* emphasized

Practice: Mice Eat Cheese

Speaking each of the following sentences should take the same amount of time. Structure words are spoken very quickly so that the rhythm of the content words is the same for each sentence.

— MICE EAT CHEESE

— The MICE EAT the CHEESE

— The MICE have EATen the CHEESE

— The MICE have been EATing the CHEESE

Basic Emphasis Pattern Structure Words (*Not* Emphasized		
pronouns (he, she)	**prepositions** (of, at, to)	**articles** (a, an, the)
"to be" verbs (is, was)	**conjunctions** (and, but)	**auxiliary verbs** (can, have, do, will)

When **content words are emphasized** and *structure words are de-emphasized*, the contrast helps the listener to hear the important words.

—From Clear Speech by Judy Gilbert.
Unit 12: Basic Emphasis Pattern: Structure Words

Practice: Cats Chase Mice

— CATS CHASE MICE

— The CATS have CHASEd the MICE

— The CATS will CHASE the MICE

— The CATS have been CHASing the MICE

— The CATS could have been CHASing the MICE

In the last sentence, "could have been" is pronounced [cuddabin] or [cud'uvbin.]

Practice: Girls Jump Rope

Formal, Clear English	Fast Casual English
GIRLS JUMP ROPE	GIRLS JUMP ROPE
The GIRLS will JUMP the ROPE	TheGIRLSul JUMP th ROPE
The GIRLS will be JUMPing the ROPE	TheGIRLSul be JUMPin'th ROPE.
The GIRLS could have been JUMPing th ROPE	TheGIRLS cud'uvbin JUMPin' th ROPE

51

Practice: Nails in a Fence

Read several times. Read quickly and smoothly.

There was a **little boy** / with a **bad temper**. / His **father** / **gave** him a **bag** of **nails** / and **told** him / that **every time** / he **lost** his **temper**, / to **hammer** a **nail** /in the **back fence**. / The **first day** / the **boy** had **driven 37 nails** / into the **fence**. / Then / it **gradually** / **dwindled down**. / He **discovered** / it was **easier** / to **hold** his **temper** / than to **drive** those **nails** / into the **fence**. /

Finally / the **day came** / when the **boy** / **didn't lose** his **temper** / at all. / He **told** his **father** / about it / and the **father suggested** / that the **boy** / <u>now</u> **pull out one nail** / for **each day** / that he was **able** / **to** hold **his** temper. / **The** days passed / and the **young boy** / **was** finally able **to tell his** father / that **all the nails** were **gone**. /

The **father took** his **son** / by the **hand** / and **led** him to the **fence**. / "You have **done well**, / **my son**, / but **look** at the **holes** / in the **fence**. / The **fence** will **never be** the **same**. / When you say **things** in **anger**, / they **leave a scar** / **just like** this one. / You can **put a knife** / in a **man** / and **draw it out**; / it **won't matter** / **how many times** / you **say** I'm **sorry**; / the **wound** is **still there**. / A **verbal wound** / is as **bad** as a **physical one**." /

Related Words

Adjective Form	Noun Form	Verb Form	Adverb Form
Angry	Anger	To anger	Angrily
Scarred	Scar	To scar	
Wounded	A wound	To wound	

Vocabulary and Related Words Chart

Temper	Noun	Mood, bad disposition, to get angry quickly
Nails, to nail [na^{y}il]	Noun, verb	That which fastens, bolt, screw
Hammer, hammer	Noun, verb	Tool for pounding
To dwindle; (down)	Verb	To decrease, to lessen
To pull out	Verb	To withdraw, to take out
Hole, holes	Noun	A cavity, an opening
Anger	Noun, verb	Rage, ire [i^{y}re], fury; to be mad
Scar, scars	Noun	Disfigurement, a mark from a wound
Knife	Noun	Cutting tool
Wound	Noun	Injury, hurt, cut
Verbal	Adjective	Spoken, oral

The Basics of Linking

All sounds within a sound unit are linked. There are several rules for linking, but here are a few simplified rules that cover most situations:

1. Linking with /y/ or /w/ glides commonly occurs when one word or syllable ends in a tense vowel or diphthong and the next word or syllable begins with a vowel.

2. When a word ending with a single consonant is followed by a word beginning with a vowel, the consonant is held and it sounds like it belongs to both words.

3. When a word or syllable ending in a consonant cluster is followed by a word beginning with a vowel, the final consonant is pronounced as if it belongs to both words.

4. When a word ends in one consonant sound and the next word begins with that same consonant sound, the sound is elongated, but is never produced twice and no extra filler sound is used.

5. The stops in English are t, d, p, k, g, and j. When a stop consonant is followed by another stop consonant in the next word, the first stop is not released and that helps the linking. The tongue is in position but before the air is released the next sound is formed. *Remember the* stops *relate to the sounds, and they may be different from the actual letters.*

6. When a word ends in a /t/ sound, followed by the word *you* or *your*, the /t/ is pronounced with a /ch/ sound. When a words ends in a /d/ sound, followed by the word *you* or *your*, the /d/ is pronounced with a /j/ or /dj/ sound.

—*From* Teaching Pronunciation: *Cambridge University Press*

Link your little fingers together. This is the way your words should link. In the sound unit, "let's get going," you should say it as one word, "Letsgetgoing!"

Here are a few examples of the simplified rules:

Examples for Rule 1: Linking with /y/ or /w/ glides commonly occurs when one word or syllable ends in a tense vowel or diphthong and the next word or syllable begins with a vowel. It also occurs across word boundaries.

/y/ Glides		/w/ Glides	
Tire	ti^{y}re	Sure	su^{w}re
Meal	me^{y}al	Oasis	o^{w}a sis
Fail	fa^{y}il	Situation	sit chew ^{w}ay shun or situ^{w}aytion
Science	sci^{y}ence	Usual	uz you ^{w}ul
Wire	wi^{y}re	Pursuaded	per su^{w}ay ded
Created	Cre^{y}ated	Poets	po^{w}ets
Fired	Fi^{y}erd	Stuart	Stu^{w}art , as in Stuart, Florida
Biopsy	Bi^{y}op sy	How is it?	ho^{w}izit??
Carry on	Carry ^{y}on	Do it	do^{w}it
Be able becomes be^{y}able		Flour	flo^{w}er

Examples for Rule 2: When a word ending with a single consonant is followed by a word beginning with a vowel, the consonant is held and it sounds like it belongs to both words.

into his arm   *look at the hole in the fence*   *mark and talk about*

Examples for Rule 3: When a word or syllable ending in a consonant cluster is followed by a word beginning with a vowel, the final consonant is pronounced as if it belongs to both words.

Years earlier   *strong and healthy*   *almost over*

Examples for Rule 4: When a word ends in one consonant or consonant cluster sound and the next word begins with that same sound, the sound is elongated, but is never produced twice and no extra filler sound is used.

Did the doctor realize   *Johnny was strong*   *with this*   *dwindled down*

Examples for Rule 5: The stops in English are t, d, p, k, g, and j. When a stop consonant sound is followed by a stop consonant sound in the next word, the first stop is not released and that helps the linking. The tongue is in position but before the air is released the next sound is formed.

A bad temper   *The first day*   *Like this one*
Blood transfusion   *had previously*   *blood to Mary.*

Examples for Rule 6: When a word ends in a /t/ sound, followed by the word *you* or *your*, the /t/ is pronounced with a /ch/ sound.

   Don't you becomes *don't cha* or *don't chew*

   Won't your becomes *won't chure*

When a words ends in a /d/ sound, followed by the word *you* or *your*, the /d/ is pronounced with a /j/ or /dj/ sound.

   Would you becomes *would juh* or *would djew*

   Did your becomes *did jer* or *did djer*

The song, *Take Me Out To The Ballgame,* includes all of the first five simplified rules of linking. Sing it out loud.

Practice: Take Me Out to the Ballgame

Rule   1
Sound   /y/
Take me out to the ball game

Rule   1   4
Sound   /y/   /th th/
Take me out with the crowd

Rule   3   5
Sound   / ts a/ /d k/
Buy me some peanuts and Cracker Jacks

Rule   5   2   5
Sound   /t k/ /f i/   /t b/
I don't care if I never get back

Rule   2
Sound   /r i/
For it's Root! Root! Root! for the home team

Rule
Sound

If they don't win, it's a shame

Rule   3   2
sound   /ts o/   /r o/
And it's One!, Two!, Three strikes, you're out!

Rule   4
Sound   /t th/
At the old ball game

Linking allows the native speaker to speak the sound units smoothly. Within each sound unit, all the words go together with no stops and no extra sounds like "uh" added.

Many of the linking examples previously cited come from the story, *For My Sister,* which follows.

Practice: For My Sister

by David C. Needham

Read the story out loud several times.

This is a **story** / of a **little boy** / **whose sister** / **needed** a **blood transfusion.** ↘/ The **doctor explained** / that she had the **same disease** / the **boy** had **recovered from** / **two years earlier.** / Her <u>only</u> **chance** at **recovery** / was a **transfusion** / from **someone**/ who had **previously** /**conquered** the **disease.** / Since the **two children** / had the **same rare blood type,** / the **boy** was the **ideal donor.** /

"**Would** you **give** your **blood** to **Mary?**" / the **doctor asked.** /

Johnny hesitated. / **His lower lip** / **started** to **tremble.** / Then he **smiled** / and said, / "Sure, / for <u>my</u> sister." /

Soon / the **two children** / were **wheeled** / into the **hospital room.** / **Mary** was **pale** and **thin.** / **Johnny** was **strong** and **healthy.** / **Neither spoke,** / but when **their eyes met,** / **Johnny smiled.** /

As the **nurse** / **inserted** the **needle** / into his **arm,** / **Johnny's smile faded.** / He **watched** his **blood** / **flow** through the **tube.** /

With the **procedure** / **almost over,** / **Johnny's voice broke** the **silence.** / He **quietly asked,** / "**Doctor,** / **when** do I **die?**" / ↘

Only then / did the **doctor realize** / why **Johnny** had **hesitated,** / why his **lip** / had **trembled** / when he **agreed** / to **donate** his **blood.** / He **thought** / **giving** his **blood** / to his **sister** / **would mean** / **giving up** <u>his</u> **life.** / In that **moment,** / he had **made** / a **great decision.** / ↘

Always end a sentence with the voice going down. ↘ *Each sound unit goes down at the end.* ↘ *Questions usually end in the voice going down.* ↘ *Yes / no questions are often taught in EFL as if the voice is to go up. That doesn't always happen in real life, unless we ask a second time and want to make sure the listener has heard use.* ↘

Linking with Phrasal Verbs

Another good example of linking can be found in phrasal verbs. Phrasal verbs contain two and three words. These are always linked together to sound almost like one word. They are very common in fast casual spoken English. Practice saying these examples.

1. To give up (something): to offer something (as a sacrifice)

    Johnny thought he would have to give up his life.   *[GIVUP^his life]*

2. To give up on (someone, something): to expect someone or something to fail

    Johnny's sister didn't give up on him.   *[GIVEUP ON ^him]*

3. To carry on: to continue

    Despite difficulties, we will carry on regardless.   *[KAREee^yon]*

4. To figure out: to understand or solve something

    Occasionally an international starts flying through his words and nothing can be figured out from that.   *[FIG^yurdOWT]*

5. To strive on: (archaic) to strive. To work very hard to attain something, and to continue to do so.

    *let us **strive on** / to **finish** the **work** we are **in**;*   *[STRIVEON]*

6. To bind up: to bandage, to tie something around a part of the body that is hurt.

    *to **bind up** the **nation's wounds***   *[BYnDUP]*

Vocabulary

1. Transfusion: The act of transferring blood or blood products to another person or animal.
2. Conquered: People or places overcome and taken by a military force.
3. To wheel: To move a person in a wheeled vehicle or on a wheeled cart.
4. To Tremble: To shake involuntarily.

Focal Words

Speakers of English often add energy, excitement and importance to our words. Not every sentence has a focal word, but many do. In the sentence: *We hold these truths to be self evident, that ALL men are created equal.* All is the focal word, and it is held a little longer as a content word, but it also goes up about half a step in pitch. This makes the melody of the language. The stressed word focuses the listener's attention, and therefore is called a *focal word.* Generally, the speaker chooses his own focus, and it can change with the speaker's emphasis

Focal Words

- A *content word* that goes up about ½ step in tone.

- *Any word that you choose* can be a focal word

- Focal words add interest, excitement and energy.

- Make a word a focal word by adding length, not volume

- In any sentence, changing the focus can change the implication

    I love shopping and eating and teaching in China (ordinary sentence)

    <u>I</u> love shopping and teaching in China (meaning me, especially))

    I **love** shopping and teaching in China (really, really enjoy)

    I love **shopping and teaching** in China (*these* are what I really like)

- Here is another example:

    I am glad that you are here today (an ordinary greeting)

    I am <u>GLAD</u> that you are here today (an *excited* greeting)

    I am glad that <u>YOU</u> are here today (because *you* are special)

    I am glad that you are <u>HERE</u> today (you chose to come *here* instead of some other engagement)

In the following story, focal words are <u>underlined.</u>

Practice: The Meanest Mother in the World

We had the **meanest mother** in the **whole world**! / While other **kids ate candy** for **breakfast**, / we had to have **cereal, eggs,** and **toast**. When **others** had a **Pepsi** and a **Twinkie** for **lunch**, / we had to **eat sandwiches**. / And / you can **guess** our **mother fixed** us a **dinner** / that was **different** from what **other kids had, too**.

Mother insisted on **knowing** / where we were at **all times**. / You'd **think** we were **convicts** in a **prison**. / She had to **know** who our **friends** were, / and what we were **doing** with them. / She **insisted** / that if we **said** we would be **gone** for an **hour**, /we would be **gone** for an **hour** or **less**.

We were **ashamed** to **admit** it, / but she had the **nerve** / to **break** the **Child Labor Laws** / by **making** us **work**. / We had to **wash** the **dishes**, / **make** the **beds**, / **learn** to **cook**, / **vacuum** the **floor**, / do **laundry**, / and **all sorts** of **cruel jobs**. / I **think** / she would **lie awake** at **night thinking** / of **more things** for us to do. / She **always insisted** on us **telling** the **truth**, / the **whole** truth, / and **nothing** but the **truth**.

By the **time** we were **teenagers**, / she could **read** our **minds**. / **Then**, / **life** was **really tough**! / **Mother wouldn't let our friends just honk** the **horn** / when they **drove up**. / They **had** to **come up** to the **door** so she could **meet** them. / While **everyone else** could **date** / when they were **12** or **13**, / we had to **wait** until we were **16**.

Because of our **mother**, / we **missed out** on **lots** of **things other kids experienced**. **None** of us have **ever** been **caught shoplifting**, / **vandalizing other's property**, / or ever **arrested** for **any crime**. / It was all her **fault**. / We **never** got **drunk**, / **took up smoking**, / **stayed out all night**, / or a **million other things**, / that **other kids did**. / **Sundays** were **reserved** for **church**, / and we **never** missed once. / We **knew better** / than to **ask** to **spend** the **night** / with a **friend** on **Saturdays**.

Now that we have **left home**, / we are **all God-fearing**, / **educated**, / **honest adults**. / We are **doing** our **best** / to be **mean** parents / **just** like Mom was. / I **think** / that's what is **wrong** / with the **world today**. / It **just doesn't** have enough **mean moms anymore**.

Vocabulary

1. **Convicts:** Prisoners or jailbirds.

2. **Twinkie:** An individual sweet cake.

3. **Cruel:** Mean and feeling no concern about it.

4. **Honk:** Blow the car horn.

5. **To have the nerve to do something:** To be brave and strong.

6. **Shoplifting:** Stealing from a store.

7. **Vandalizing:** Deliberately destroy or damage property.

Pronunciation Practice for Past Tense Regular Verbs

/t/	/d/		/ed/	
Fixed	Ashamed	Experienced	Insisted	
Missed	Stayed out	Reserved	Arrested	Educated

Linking with /y/ Glides	Linking with /w/ glides
Cereal [Cere^{y}al]	Cruel [cru^{w}el]
Experienced [experi^{y}enced]	Who our [who^{w}our

Pace or Rate of Speaking

- 130 words per minute (wpm) is slow

- 150-180 words per minute is normal

- 180-220 words per minute is fast

- Speak at a normal rate – not too fast and not too slow

- Sound units, linking, and rhythm are the keys to speaking at the normal rate

Frequently Internationals speak so slowly and jerkily that the native English speaker cannot understand them or perhaps does not have the patience to wait for each word. It is important to have an idea of the normal speaking rate for North American English.

- 130 words per minute (wpm) is slow. If a native speaker finishes a sentences for an international, the utterance is generally too slow.

- 150-180 wpm is the normal rate of speaking. Think of the TV commercials. Every 15 seconds, we see a new commercial. That means about 40-45 words can be said in just a quarter of a minute. This paragraph has that many words.

- 180-220 wpm is a fast pace for English. We use this rate when we are excited and have a lot to say in a few words.

The goal is 150-180 wpm. Occasionally an international starts flying through the words and nothing can be figured out from that. For some, English sounds so rapid, and the international tries to sound like an American. To learn, first get all the elements in order and then work to speak at the normal speed. Also, learners might fluctuate between too slow or too fast until finally using the correct rate of speaking.

CAUTION: Speaking too fast is not English!!!! Sound unit breaks, breath pauses, linking and rhythm are ABSOLUTELY NECESSARY!!!

Practice: The Bill of Rights

The **Bill** of **Rights**, / **explained here** in **simple terms**, / is **also known** / as the **first 10 amendments** / to the **Constitution** / of the **United States**. / **Many** of **these amendments** / **seek** to **protect** the **rights** of **citizens** / by **focusing** on **personal freedoms** / and the **power of government.** / The **amendments included** in the **Bill** of **Rights** are:

1. **Congress cannot make** a **law** / that **affects** the **establishment** / of **religion,** / **restricts** a **person's right** / or the **press's right** to **free speech,** / or **restricts** the **right** of **people** / to **gather together** in a **peaceful manner**.

    - Freedom of religion

    - Freedom of speech

    - Freedom of the press

    - Freedom of assembly

2. **Citizens have** the **right** to **own guns**.

3. **During times** of **peace** / **soldiers cannot take up residence** / in **someone else's house** without that **owner's permission**.

4. A **person,** / his **house** and **belongings** / **cannot be searched** / or **taken,** / and he **cannot be given** a **warrant** / without **good reason**.

5. You **cannot be tried** for a **serious crime** / without a **Grand Jury deciding** / there is **enough evidence** for a **trial**.

6. A **person should be given** a **speedy** / and **public trial** / by a **jury** of his **peers** / in the **state** and **district** / where he **committed** the **crime**.

7. A **person** has the **right** to a **jury** in a civil case where **more** than **$20** is **being disputed**.

8. **Excessive bail** and/or **fines** shall **not be ordered,** / and **cruel** and **unusual punishments** / **can't be imposed**.

9. You have **rights** / **beyond** those / **listed** in the **Constitution**.

10. **Areas** and **laws** that **aren't governed** or **prohibited directly** by the **Constitution** may be **made** by **individual states**.

Vocabulary

1. **Bill:** Here it means law.

2. **Amendments:** An article added to the US Constitution.

3. **Restrict:** To put a limit on something.

4. **Permission:** Consent. Agreement.

5. **Warrant:** A document issued by a government official allowing the police or some other body to make an arrest or search the home, apartment or office.

6. **Grand Jury:** A jury of 23 people selected to examine the validity or truth of an accusation before a trial.

7. **Peers:** a person of about the same age, status.

8. **To dispute:** To argue about something.

9. **Excessive bail:** Charging more than usual to be temporarily released from jail before the trial.

10. **Prohibited:** Forbidden. Banned. Just don't do it.

Voice Quality

- Every Language has a unique voice quality.

- Make your English sound like a native speaker, not like Chinglish or Spanglish, etc., Those are not languages.

- Sound like me.

- You speak your native language in one part of your brain, and a second language in another part.

The language simply must sound like English. Each language has its own voice quality setting (VQS). In fact, the VQS for British English is a little different from NAE. Here simply make sure the spoken English sounds native. Work to form an English voice, rather than overlay the native voice quality on top of English words. Discourage Chinglish, Spanglish, Hindglish, etc. These mixed voiced qualities make clarity almost impossible. In addition, these overlays or heavy accents require concentrated listening. Native speakers generally will exercise concentrated listening about 90 seconds before finding something else to do or someone else to do the task. A person speaks the native or heart language in one part of the brain and the language learner must develop the new language in another part of the brain.

Practice: Today's Teacher

After being interviewed by the **school administration,** / the **eager teaching prospect said:** / "**Let** me **see** if I've **got** this **right.** / You **want** me to **go** / into that **room** / with **all those kids,** / and **fill** their **every waking moment** / with a **love** for **learning.** / **And** I'm **supposed** / to **instill** a **sense** of **pride** / in their **ethnicity,** / **modify disruptive behavior,** / **observe** them for **signs** of **abuse** / and <u>**even**</u> **censor** / their **tee-shirt messages** / and **dress habits.**

You **want** me to **wage** a **war** on **drugs** / and **sexually transmitted diseases,** / **check** their **backpacks** / for **weapons** of **mass destruction,** / and **raise** their **self esteem.** / You **want** me to **teach** them **patriotism,** / **good citizenship,** /

sportsmanship, / fair play, / how to **register** to **vote**, / how to **balance** a **checkbook**, / and how to **apply** for a **job**.

I am to **check** their **heads** for **lice**, / **maintain** a **safe environment**, / **recognize signs** of **anti-social behavior**, / **offer advice**, / **write letters** of **recommendation** / for **student employment** and **scholarships**, / **encourage respect** for the **cultural diversity** of **others**, / and **oh**, / **make sure** / that I **give** the **girls** in my **class** / **fifty percent** of my **attention**.

My **contract requires** me to **work** / on my **own time** / after **school**, / **evenings** and **weekends** / **grading papers**. / **Also**, / I must **spend** my **summer vacation** / at my **own expense** / **working** toward **advance certification** / and a **Masters degree**. / And on my **own time** / you **want** me to **attend committee** / and **faculty meetings**, / **PTA meetings**, / and **participate** in **staff development training**.

I am to be a **paragon** of **virtue**, / **larger** than **life**, / such that my **very presence** / will **awe** my **students** / into being **obedient** / and **respectful** of **authority**. / And I am to **pledge allegiance** / to **family values** / and this **current administration**.

You **want** me to **incorporate technology** / into the **learning experience**, / **monitor web sites**, / and **relate personally** with each **student**. / That **includes** / **deciding** who might be **potentially dangerous**/ **and**/or **liable** *to* **commit** a **crime** in **school**. / I am to **make sure all students** / **pass** the **mandatory state exams**, / even those who **don't come** to **school regularly** / or **complete any** of their **assignments**.

Plus, / I am to **make sure** / that **all** of the **students** with **handicaps** / **get** an **equal education** / **regardless** of the **extent** / of their **mental** or **physical handicap**. / And I am to **communicate regularly** / with the **parents** by **letter**, / **telephone**, / **email**, / **newsletter** / and **report card**.

All of this I am to **do**/ with **just** a **piece of chalk**, / a **computer**, / a **few books**, / a **bulletin board**, / a **big smile** / **AND** / on a **starting salary** / that **qualifies** my **family** for **food stamps**!

And you **wonder** / **why** I **need** to **PRAY?**"

Tone

English is a low-pitched, non-tonal language. Other languages that are tonal use the same word, such as *Ba* with high, low or shifting tones to mean uniquely different words. Any tone in NAE used to say *Help!* still comes out *Help!* Regardless of saying an utterance low, or high, or sliding down to up, it is still the same word.

Internationals who use the high tones of their native language in speaking English face a type of prejudice not often discussed. In addition, tone of voice matters in English. Men who speak in high, breathy tones are considered weak. Women who speak the same way are considered difficult to get along with. Americans generally don't even know why "that person grates on my nerves," but it often is the fact that the tones are out of the NAE normal, low voiced range. The females in North America speak with a lower tone than males in many tonal groups outside of North America, although Arabic speakers are even lower in their tone of voice.

Voices should go down in tone at the end of a sound unit and at the end of each sentence. In addition avoid using "up-speak" at the end of an utterance. ↘

Tone and Volume in English

- Chinese and some other languages are tonal; English is not.
- English is medium or low toned, but not as low as Arabic.
- In English, when in doubt, always go low and down in tone.
- Volume in English is in the middle of world languages.
- Power English is used by people in control, just as power is used in other languages by people in control.
- Power English is not loud, but assured and passionate

English is about mid-way on the volume chart of international languages. Other languages such as Arabic are louder. However, many languages require less volume and air than English does. The rule of thumb is for the learner to match volume for volume, except in cases of argument. Then a person should get quieter to diffuse the misunderstanding.

Listen and try to speak at the normal volume for American English. Both too loud and too soft-spoken are out of English normal range. Speakers who are consistently too soft end up being ineffectual in management and office relationships. Their opinions are seen as unsure, and thus ignored or not given credence.

If too loud, their opinions are seen as pushy or obnoxious, and often resented. Normal volume is important. Have them listen to a TV sitcom, and see how the volume matches, rises, and falls, as each person uses volume to get what they desire.

Go down in tone ↘ at the end of phrases and sentences. ↘

Practice: Stopping by Woods on a Snowy Evening

Whose **woods** these are / I **think** I **know**.
His **house** is in the **village though**;
He will **not see** me **stopping** here
To **watch** his **woods** / **fill up** with **snow**. ↘

Read it quietly and with the feeling of beauty, but also of weariness.

My **little horse must think** it **queer**
To **stop** without a **farmhouse near**
Between the **woods** and **frozen lake**
The **darkest evening** of the **year**. ↘

He **gives** his **harness bells** / a **shake**
To **ask** / if there is **some mistake**.
The **only other sound's** the **sweep**
Of **easy wind** and **downy flake**. ↘

The woods are **lovely, / dark and deep**,
But I have **promises** to **keep**,
And **miles** to **go** before I **sleep**,
And **miles** to **go** before I **sleep**. ↘

—Robert Frost (This work is now in the public domain)

On the surface, this poem is simplicity itself. The speaker is **stopping by** some **woods on a snowy evening**. He or she takes in the lovely scene in near-silence, is tempted to stay longer, but acknowledges the pull of obligations and the considerable distance yet to be traveled before he or she can rest for the night.

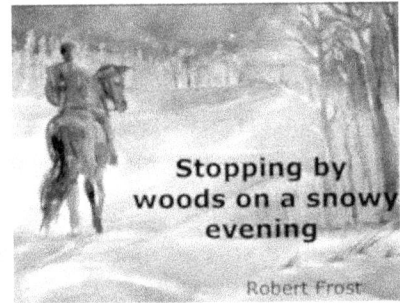

Stopping by woods on a snowy evening

Robert Frost

Robert Frost's poem, ***Stopping by Woods on a Snowy Evening*** is rich in figurative language. It contains **symbolism**. The village, the journey and the **woods symbolize** civilization, life's journey, and death, respectively.

Speaking with Expression

Speak English with the same life and joy that you speak any first or heart language. Expression is what helps us read emotion and mood into the language.

Remember the school librarian who could read a story so vividly that every child could picture the action. That is reading with expression. Our speaking should be alive as well. Avoid monotones and put life into your speech.

Emotions, Feelings, and Energy

- When one speaks with emotion, feeling and energy, it helps listeners to "read between the lines"
- Body language is, to some extent, unique for each language.
- Feelings are understood from body language.
- English is an energetic language.
- It is exhausting to speak a second language.
- Be a great actor and make your English sound alive today.

Practice: Blood, Sweat, and Tears Speech

—Sir Winston Churchill, May 13th 1940

On **Friday evening last** / I **received** from **His Majesty** / the **mission** / to **form** a **new administration.** / It was the **evident will** of **Parliament** / and the **nation** / that this should be **conceived** on the **broadest possible basis** / and that it should **include** <u>all</u> **parties.**

I have <u>**already**</u> **completed** / the **most important part** of this **task.** / A **war cabinet** has been **formed** of **five members,** / **representing,** / with the **Labour, Opposition,** / and **Liberals,** / the **unity** of the **nation.** / It was **necessary** / that this should be **done** / in <u>**one single day**</u> /on **account** of the **extreme urgency** / and **rigor** of **events.** / **Other key positions** were **filled yesterday.** / I am **submitting** a **further list** / to the **king** <u>**tonight**</u>. / I **hope** to **complete** the **appointment** / of **principal ministers** during **tomorrow.** / The **appointment** of <u>**other**</u> **ministers** <u>**usually**</u> takes a **little longer.** /

I **trust** / when **Parliament meets** <u>**again**</u> / this **part** of my **task** will be **completed** / and / that the **administration** will be **complete** in <u>**all**</u> **respects.** / I **considered** it in the **public interest** / to **suggest** to the **Speaker** / that the **House** should be **summoned today.** / At the **end** of **today's proceedings,** / the **adjournment** of the **House** / will be **proposed** / until **May 21**/ with **provision** for **earlier meeting** / if **need be.** / **Business** for that / will be **notified** to **MPs** / at the **earliest opportunity.** / I <u>**now**</u> **invite** the **House** / by a **resolution** / to **record** its **approval** of the **steps taken** / and **declare** its **confidence** in the **new government.** / The **resolution:** / "That this **House** <u>**welcomes**</u> / the **formation** of a **government** / **representing the united** / and **inflexible resolve** of the **nation** / to **prosecute** the **war** with **Germany** / to a **victorious conclusion."** /

To **form** an **administration** of this <u>**scale**</u> / and <u>**complexity**</u> / is a **serious undertaking** in itself. / But we are in the **preliminary phase** / of **one** of the **greatest battles** in **history.** / We are in **action** / at **many other points—** / in **Norway** and in **Holland—** / and we <u>**have**</u> to be <u>**prepared**</u> in the **Mediterranean.** / The **air battle** is **continuing,** / and <u>**many**</u> **preparations** / have to be **made here** at **home.** / In this **crisis** / I **think** I may be **pardoned** / if 1 do <u>**not**</u> address the **House** / at **any length today,** / and I **hope** / that **any** of **my friends** / and **colleagues** / or **former colleagues** / who are **affected** by the **political reconstruction** / will **make**

all allowances / for **any lack** of **ceremony** / with which it has been **necessary** to **act.** /

I **say** to the **House** / as I **said** to **ministers** / who have **joined** this **government,** / I have **nothing** to **offer** but **blood,** / **toil, tears,** / and **sweat.** / We have before us / an **ordeal** of the **most grievous kind.** / We have before us **many,** / **many months** / of **struggle** and **suffering.** / You **ask,** / **what** is **our policy?** / I **say** it is to **wage war** by **land,** / **sea,** / and **air.** / **War** with **all our might** / and with **all** the **strength God** has **given us,** / and to **wage war** / against a **monstrous tyranny never surpassed** in the **dark** / and **lamentable catalogue** of **human crime.** /

That is **our policy.** / You **ask,** / **what** is **our aim?** / I can **answer** in **one word.** / It is **victory.** / **Victory** at **all costs** — / **Victory** in **spite** of **all terrors** — / **Victory,** / however **long** and **hard** the **road** may be, / for without **victory** / there is **no** **survival.** / Let that be **realized.** / **No survival** for the **British Empire,** / **no survival** for **all** that the **British Empire** has **stood for,** / **no survival** for the **urge,** / the **impulse** of the **ages,** / that **mankind** shall **move forward** toward his **goal.** / I **take up my task** in **buoyancy** and **hope.** / I **feel sure** / that **our cause** will **not be suffered** / to **fail among men.** / I **feel entitled** at **this juncture,** / at **this time,** / to **claim** the **aid** of **all** / and to **say,** / "**Come then,** / **let us go forward together** / with **our united strength.**"

Scenario for Churchill's speech: Great Britain is at war with Germany in 1939 / and the Germans are bombing England. / The evacuation / of British soldiers from Norway / is underway / ending on May 2, 1940. / Neville Chamberlain resigns as Prime Minister / and Winston Churchill takes the job. / This is his famous war-time speech.

Word Count is 745 words. If the normal rate of speaking is 150 words per minute (wpm), then this should take the speaker only 5 minutes. It can take a little longer with Power English, Focal Words, Energy and Emphasis.

Read the *Blood, Tears and Sweat* speech aloud many times.

The rate of speaking English can be improved for the slow or hesitant learner, and made steady by beginning slowly, and repeating faster each time.

Power English

Speaking with control, authority, capability and the depth of conviction defines power oratory or speaking. A successful teacher, manager, public speaker and many others use the power of their voice to gain results they desire.

All languages have leaders who speak with authority. Don't all mothers speak to their children with power in their voices? Speak the following with power English:

The powers that be / are the powers / who speak with authority.

Are you speaking with trepidation? That reveals unease, anxiety, nervousness, fear or apprehension, and you should practice and develop a stronger voice that has authority. It is risky to speak a new language. But, it will help the student in the workplace and in life in this country.

Power is often exercised using volume. If you are the president of a company, volume is particularly important, either soft or strong. You can learn to speak or issue commands without being offensive or obnoxious. Speaking with authority is necessary in any language. It doesn't have to be loud to be powerful!

Task: Look at the paragraphs above and determine where you would place the sound unit marks would be placed if you were speaking the words.

Clarity and Intelligibility in Speaking

The words in a sentence must be clearly spoken. Leaving out syllables or not pronouncing the last consonants in a word make the listener have to concentrate hard on what is being spoken. This stops the comprehension of the listener while the speaker continues talking. So communication is broken. All the syllables in English are important. That means hearing the endings of regular past tense verbs and the endings of plurals matter. These endings must be heard as we link the words within a sound unit, and at the end of the sentence.

Choral Reading for Stamina

We read passages orally to develop *stamina* in speaking. Reading aloud teaches the brain how English should actually sound.

Code Switching

Code switching happens when an individual wants to speak on the proper "wavelength" of the person with whom they are speaking. For example, a mother speaks differently to her child than to her child's teacher. We all unconsciously code-switch many times a day. For example, my niece told me to speak "normal," not like a schoolteacher, when I came to visit her. Often monolingual speakers vary the level of formality in their speech depending on to whom they are speaking.

Communication

A **University of Pennsylvania study** reported that the majority of **communication** is transmitted non-verbally.

- 70% of **communication** is body language (facial expressions, clothing and outside appearance, body movements)

- 23% is voice tone and inflection (are you sounding angry, happy, concerned, serious, questioning?

- And only 7% is your spoken words!

The goal is to have your *non-verbal* message match your verbal message.

Physical behaviors, not necessarily words, are frequently used in speaking. Most people use facial expressions and hand movements when talking to others, and many people even do so while talking on a phone. This is an unconscious action when a speaker is using their native language, but may not do so when speaking in a second language.

It is important to learn to use physical movements that native speakers use. They may differ from those in a different language. These movements include eye movement, touch, the use of space and smiles, grimaces and other movements. If you are happy, in English, you should look happy. A small or large smile conveys a lot of information.

Eye contact is really important when conversing with English speakers. Eye contact includes a cultural judgment on the person. Idioms and statements in English, such as "He won't even look me in the eye," include an unconscious judgment that the person is hiding something, is lying or is ashamed. Eye contact is necessary and shows interest and attention to the person. The eye contact goes back and forth in a conversation.

Also studies have shown that eye contact both opens and closes conversation and meetings. It shows confidence and in some cases, even dominance. As you attentively listen and have eye contact, avoid staring which comes with not blinking and makes the other person feel uneasy. For beginners in eye contact, it is hard to decide how much and how long to maintain eye contact.

In speaking or making a speech, be sure to use the Eiffel Tower stance. It helps to keep you from swaying back and forth as often happens when standing with both feet tightly together. Instead stand with feet about 10 inches apart. That gives you a good foundation, and also helps you avoid clinging or holding onto the podium, table or speakers' stand.

Accent Correction

Learning to speak with clarity as a native English speaker is hard, but it can be done and is done. Improving clarity comes after the **decision** to accomplish several things. Here are some hints:

Actually **listen** to the way the native speaks, and begin to develop a voice quality that matches that sound.

Begin to **read** widely. Decide to go from intermediate to advanced to fluent. There are no books or lessons generally available for this. It seems to come from the discipline, intent and desire of the individual. Simple learning how to correctly say the consonants, vowels and words is foundational, but will not complete movement from advanced to fluent. Fluency has its own big requirements to accomplish, like power English, stamina in speaking, and body language, to name a few.

Reading helps with vocabulary, grammar and general knowledge.

Quietly begin to **collect and use** the useful idioms you may yourself hear. For example, when a friend gets angry with another person, and says, "She gets under my skin!" then find out what that really means. Get a good Advanced Dictionary for ESL and look it up under the word, "skin." Or simply look up the phrase on line.

Ask someone you feel safe with a lot of the questions you might have. Hopefully, your friend or teacher can mentor and encourage.

If you get angry at being laughed at or frequently asked to repeat, **decide** to over-learn and clarify until that no longer happens. The story is told of the Colombian woman's anger at being told she was "cute" because of her way of speaking. That caused her to enunciate and to grow in determination to conquer the language. It can also happen to the person who is asked repeatedly to "say it again or write that down for me."

Listen seriously to music and musical phrases. Get sing-a-long disk or the words off the internet and begin to use the music to make the correct rhythm of the language.

Work at being able to mentally code switch to the different dialects. Think how the educated and the uneducated talk and work to understand both. What is the difference between, "Can I help you?" and "Yeh. Whatchawant?"

Learn the compressions, reductions, and fast informal speech of English. It has rules, too. Get a book like "Whaddaysay" by Nina Weinsten and expect people to sound like that.

Develop an ability to guess correctly as to what is about to come next. Learn some of the English collocations, like salt and pepper.

Don't just watch the movies. Listen to the movies! **Hear** the way the native actually says certain sentences and repeat that. Listen to the same movie many times.

Watch the mouths of the native speakers and also watch for the wrinkles around their mouths. The wrinkles match the language. **Use** the muscles that fit the language and you will develop a set of muscles for each language you speak.

Try a little acting. Make voices and imitate the way the native speaks; wear a mental mask and pretend you are the actor.

Find a class and learn. An Oral Production class helps with clarity and all the elements of accent reduction.

Obviously the learner is ultimately responsible for the degree of learning that will take place. The teacher is a facilitator and encourager, but not the answer to the determination that must take place. Only the learner can decide to change.

Compression and Reduction

Fast Casual English	Formal English
Whatcha Got?	**What Have You Got?**
Whatcha got in yer hand?	What have you got in your hand?
I donno. A thingamajig, I guess.	I don't know. A thingamajig, I guess.
Whatsa thingamajig? Ya gotta tell me.	What is a thingamajig? You have got to tell me.
Its somethin' I donno the name of.	It is something I do not know the name of.
Whaddaya call it?	What do you call it?
I donno. A whatchamacallit, I guess.	I don't know. A what you might call it, I guess.
Well, handit here.	Well, give it to me.
No. I gotta use it.	No. I have to use it.
Whatcha gonna do with it?	What are you going to do with it?
Fix the doorknob.	Fix the doorknob.
Can ya fix stuff?	Can you fix various things?
Sure.	Sure.

Vocabulary

A thingamajig: This is used for things whose names one has forgotten or simply don't know.

Informal words used for the unknown or forgotten name of a person or thing.

Whatsit	Whatchamacallit	Doodad
Thinguhmubob	Thingamajig	Doohickey
Gizmo	Widget	Gadget

Compressions

The following is a compression built on Carolyn Graham's Jazz Chant, *You Ought To Call Your Mother*.

Practice: Ya Oughta Call Yer mother.

Ya oughta call yer mother.
    I'm gonna.
When'er ya gonna call 'er?
    Soon.
He oughta write 'is brother.
    He's gonna.
When'ze gonna write 'em?
    Won't be long.
She ought call 'er mother.
    She'll get around to it.
When're ya gonna call yer family.
    Before long.

This is a round wooden coin that is a joke item available in some gift shops

If someone tells you they will do something when they "get around to it," you simply give them *a round tuit*, and say "OK, now do it!"

Vocabulary: Procrastination

	Procrastination [pro cras tuh NA shun}.
	When I get around to it.
	It won't be long now.
	In a little while
	Before too long
	In a few weeks
	Sometime soon
	Whenever.

Practice: Compressions

Read the following pairs outloud. The second sentence in each pair is more casual and contains more compressions and linking.

You don't have to be able to speak these compressions,
Ya' don hafta be able ta speak these compressions,

but you've got to be able to understand them.
bucha've gotta be able ta understand 'um.

—*Unknown Author*

Practice: Fishing

from *Import,* an in-house publication of the Port of Seattle.

"Hiyamac."	Hi, Mac.
"Lobuddy."	Hello, Buddy.
"Binnearlong?"	Been here long?
"Cupplours."	A couple of hours.
"Ketchenenny?"	Are you catching any fish?
"Goddafew."	Got a few.
"Kindarthey?"	What kind are they?
"Bassencarp."	Bass and Carp.
"Ennysizetoom?"	Any size to them?
"Cuplapowns."	A couple of pounds.
"Hittinhard?"	Are they hitting hard?
"Sordalike."	Sort of. Maybe.
"Wahchoozin?"	What are you using?
"Gobbaworms."	A gob of worms. (lot of)
"Fishanonaboddum?"	Are you fishing on the bottom?
"Rydonaboddum."	Right down on the bottom.
"Whatchadrinkin?"	What are you drinking?
"Cupahotchoklit."	A cup of hot chocolate.
"Igoddago."	I have got to go.
"Seeyouaroun'."	See you around.
"Yeahtakideezy."	Yes, take it easy.
"Gudluk."	Good luck.

Dialogue Not Monologue - Speaking North American Style

Conversational Ballgames

Handling conversation in a Western or NAE way is like two people playing tennis. One of them (the server) introduces a topic (the conversational ball), and after a few sentences, they hit it over the net to the other person (or wait for the other person to comment.)

If that person agrees, they can add something to the topic or elaborate further; if that person disagrees, they can question, challenge, or state a position. Then the ball is returned (hit back) to the server.

The server is happy because you returned the conversational ball, and can comment, agree, disagree, or elaborate, the again hit it back over the net.

They continue speaking briefly and passing the ball back to the other until the conversation ends (the game is over.)

The object of the dialogue (game) is to speak back and forth. Keep the topic in play or give yourself a way to go to another topic or to speak to others.

Don't monopolize the conversation. It should not be a lecture.

It is NOT a monologue!!! Everyone must get a chance to speak at least a few sentences.

Task: *Icebreaker*

Get into small groups. Discuss the topic of Hurricanes.

1. How frequent are hurricanes or typhoons in your country?

2. What preparations should you make for yourself, your place of work or for your family?

3. Do you have a special place to go for safety?

Oral Speaking Evaluation

The Oral Evaluation is useful as you think about how you actually speak English. It can show areas you have accomplished in the spoken language, and show weaknesses you can still work on.

The first line concerns use of sound units while speaking. If you use the language correctly, you will be using sound units. Take those nano-breaths that help you and the listener. If you are running though the sentences, or observe the listener with a puzzled look, it might just mean you are not taking the time you need. You can grade yourself from a number 1 meaning doing poorly, or a number 4or 5 meaning you have accomplished this task in oral English.

As you evaluate and questions yourself about all the steps on the evaluation, you can also ask a native speaker to help you. In general, the native speaker is not trained in helping with English Language Learners (ELL). So many do not know these terms. They just learned it as a native.

ORAL SPEAKING EVALUATION CHECKLIST

1.	Sound Units uh, like, uh, etc.	5	4	3	2	1	Broken English, hesitation sounds
2.	Linking words in phrases	5	4	3	2	1	Wrong pausing in speaking
3.	Focal words	5	4	3	2	1	Personal emphasis used correctly.
4.	Stress: word, phrase, sentence	5	4	3	2	1	Emphasis wrong, leads to misunderstanding
5.	Single sound reproduction	5	4	3	2	1	Substitutes or garbles sounds
6.	Syllables	5	4	3	2	1	Omits or garbles certain syllables
7.	Pace Rate of speaking	5	4	3	2	1	Much too slow/fast. Long or no pauses between words
8.	Tone: Native English low	5	4	3	2	1	Out of English range high / low
9.	Volume Control	5	4	3	2	1	Too soft, breathy too noisy and demanding
10.	Speaking with expression of emotions & feelings	5	4	3	2	1	Robot-like; sounds dis-interested, monotone
11.	Breath control native-like	5	4	3	2	1	Jerky & awkward; makes listener lose train of thought
12	Energy level	5	4	3	2	1	Lazy, too tired, not English
13	Stamina	5	4	3	2	1	Ability to speak at length
14	Power English	5	4	3	2	1	No authority in voice. Sounds timid.
15	Body Language	5	4	3	2	1	Facial expressions and body movements
16.	Clarity and Intelligibility	5	4	3	2	1	Understanding zero to understanding all elements.

5 is excellent, 1 is poor. This will show you the areas that need the most work.

MORE FUN PRACTICES

Practice: Silent Letters

> Knife and a fork / bottle and a cork
>> Fleas and Gnats / on Dogs and Cats.

This is a nonsensical rhyme, but contains two words with silent letters: The K in Knife and the G in gnats are not spoken.

> Pronounce Bottle as BAAA dl or BAAA dul.

> Pronounce Knife as Nife.

> Pronounce Gnats as Nats. Gnats are tiny insects.

> Rhyming words: Fork and Cork, Gnats and cats.

Practice: Slit the Sheet

> I **slit** the **sheet**,
>> the **sheet** I **slit**,
>
> and on the **slitted sheet**
>> I **sit**.

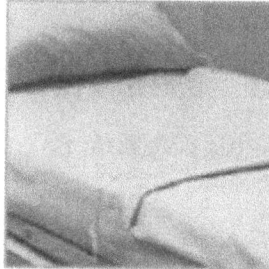

sheet

slit

Vocabulary

1. **Slit:** (verb) To make a long, narrow cut in something.

To pronounce sheet, remember to hold the eeeeee sound the length of time it takes to stretch a rubber band out full length, or to open your hand completely and hold the fingers stretched completely out.

The /i/ in slit and sit are short vowels. Make a slicing motion with your hand as you say it. It is the same sound as found in *Is it in the ship?*

85

Practice: B As in Biscuit

The following is an old diction test for would-be radio announcers, "To be read clearly, without mistakes, in less than 20 seconds."

—from Coronet Magazine, August 1948).

I **bought** a **bit** of **baking powder** /and **baked** a **batch** of **biscuits.** / I **brought** a **big basket** / of **biscuits** / **back** to the **bakery** /and **baked a basket** of **big biscuits.**

Then / I **took** the **big basket of biscuits** / and the **basket** of **big biscuits** / and **mixed** the **big biscuits** / with the **basket** of **biscuits** / that was **next** to the **big basket** / and **put** a **bunch** of **biscuits** / from the **basket** into a **biscuit mixer** / and **brought** the **basket of biscuits** / and the **box** of **mixed biscuits** / and the **biscuit mixer** / to the **bakery** / and **opened** a **tin** of **sardines.**

Sounds: Over emphasize the endings.

    Bought   Bit   Baked   Batch   Brought   Big   Basket   Biscuits

Past tense endings of Regular Verbs: Baked /t/; Mixed /t/; opened /d/

Vocabulary

1. **Batch:** A quantity produced at one time.

2. **Tin:** A can of sardines

3. **Items:**
   A big basket
   Regular biscuits
   Big biscuits
   Biscuit mixer
   Box of mixed biscuits, both large and regular sized.

Practice: Letters That Say Their Name

2 Y's U R.	Too wise you are
2 Y's U B.	Too wise you be
I C U R.	I see you are
2 Y's 4 me!	Too wise for me!

L8 4 work   Late for work.

Practice: Betty Botter's Butter

Betty Botter bought some butter / **but, said** she, / the **butter's bitter.**
If I **put it in my batter,** / it will **make my batter bitter.**
But a **bit of <u>better</u> butter** / will **make my bitter batter better.**
So she **bought some better butter,** / **better** than the **bitter butter,**
  put it in her **bitter batter,** / **made** her **bitter batter better.**
So 'twas **better** / **Betty Botter** / **bought some better butter.**

The Flap /d/ Rule

Betty [Beh dee]	Botter [Bah der]	Better [Beh der]
Butter [buh der]	Bitter [bih der]	Batter [bah der]

Practice: She Sells Sea Shells

Working on the /s/ and /sh/ sounds.

> She **sells seashells** / on the **seashore**.
> The **shells** she **sells** are **seashells**, / I'm sure.
> And / if she **sells seashells** / on the **seashore**,
> Then I'm **sure** / she **sells seashore shells**.

Pronunciation: Sure [shoe were] say the words shoe and were very rapidly.

Practice: Through Tough Thoughts

Read this sentence:
English can be **understood / through tough thorough thought, / though**.

Through [thru]; Tough [tuhf]; Thorough [thur ow]; Thought [thaw t]; Though [thow].

Vocabulary

1. **Tough**: [tuf]: Strong. Can hold up under difficult conditions. *Learning English can be tough for many speakers.*

2. **Through**: [threw]: Moving from one side to the other.

3. **Thorough**: [ther rō]: Complete in every detail. Carefully and completely.

4. **Thought**: [thaw t]: Action of thinking. *Don't give it another thought.*

5. **Though**: [thō]: However, or although. *He will be here, though he will be late.*

Practice: Sit in Solemn Silence

To **sit** in **solemn silence** / in a **dull, dark dock,**
In a **pestilential prison,** / with a **life-long lock,**
Awaiting the **sensation** / of a **short, sharp shock,**
From a **cheap** and **chippy chopper** / on a **big black block!**

To **sit** in **solemn silence** / in a **dull, dark dock,**
In a **pestilential prison,** / with a **life-long lock,**   [pes tuh len chul]
Awaiting the **sensation** / of a **short, sharp shock,**
From a **cheap** and **chippy chopper** / on a **big black block!**

A **dull, dark dock,** / a **life-long lock,,**
A **short, sharp shock,** / a **big black block!**
To **sit** in **solemn silence** / in a **pestilential prison,**
And / **awaiting** the **sensation** / of a **short sharp shock**
From a **cheap** and **chippy chopper** / on a **big black block!**

—From Act I of the 1885 Gilbert and Sullivan Opera, The Mikado

Scenario: The three characters think about the execution of one of them. The Emperor has decided that the town is behind on their executions, and a beheading must occur immediately. Sung by the three people who might be executed.

Using **Alliteration** [Uh lit ter rā shun]: Using the same letter or sound at the beginning of adjacent or closely connected words.

Examples: dull, dark dock; pestilential prison; life-long lock, short, sharp shock cheap, chippy, chopper; big black block; Sit in solemn silence.

Vocabulary

1. **Solemn:** Quiet and serious. Very dignified.

2. **Dock:** Enclosure in a criminal court. *In the dock* is the usual phrase.

3. **Pestilential:** [pes tuh lent shul]: Relating to an infectious disease.

4. **Cheap and chippy chopper:** A knife for beheading someone.

5. **Big black block:** The chopping block for executions of long ago.

Practice: Woodchuck

Ch's and Wo's

How much wood / could Chuck Woods' woodchuck chuck, / if Chuck Woods' woodchuck could / and would chuck wood?

 If Chuck Woods' woodchuck could / and would chuck wood, / how much wood could / and would Chuck Woods' woodchuck chuck?

Vocabulary

1. **To chuck something:** To throw something or to discard something. *Oh, just chuck it, I don't need it anymore.*

Woodchucks and **Groundhogs** / are the **same animal.** / We **celebrate Groundhog Day** on **February Second.** / **Very early** in the **morning,** / **reporters** and **observers travel** to **Pennsylvania** / to **discover** if **Punxsutawney [punk suh taw nee] Phil,** / the **best known prognosticator [praag naa stuh kay tr],** / will or will **not see** his **shadow.** / This **weather prediction tradition** / **goes back several hundred years.** / If it is a **sunny day** / and he **sees his shadow,** / that **foretells six more weeks** of **winter weather.** / If it is a **cloudy day,** / it **means** an **early spring** is **coming.**

Groundhog Day / is **also** an **astronomical [as tro nom mi cul] holiday.** / It is the **day** between the **solstice [saal stuhs],** / December 21st or 22nd, / and the **equinox [ee kwuh naaks],** / March 20th or 21st. / The **equinoxes, [ee kwuh naak suhz]/ solstices [saal stuh suhz]/** and **cross-quarter days** / are **events** that **take place** / in **Earth's orbit** around **the sun.**

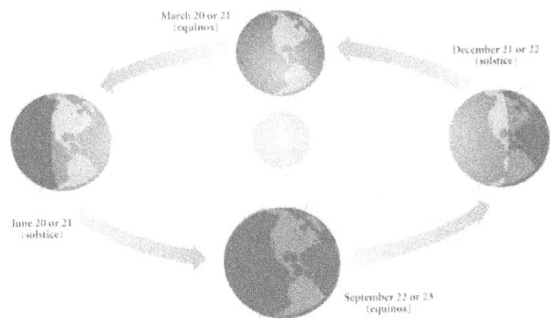

—found on Google with no attribution

Practice: English Language Idiosyncrasies

For those who reed and right   (read and write)

We'll begin with a box, and the plural is boxes;
> but the plural of ox became oxen not oxes.
> One fowl is a goose, but two are called geese,
> yet the plural of moose should never be meese.
> You may find a lone mouse or a nest full of mice;
> yet the plural of house is houses, not hice.

If the plural of man is always called men,
> why shouldn't the plural of pan be called pen?
> If I spoke of my foot and show you my feet,
> and I give you a boot, would a pair be called beet?
> If one is a tooth and a whole set are teeth, why
> shouldn't the plural of booth be called beeth?

Then one may be that, and three would be those,
> yet hat in the plural would never be hose,
> and the plural of cat is cats, not cose.
> We speak of a brother and also of brethren,
> but though we say mother, we never say methren.
> Then the masculine pronouns are he, his and him,
> but imagine the feminine, she, shis and shim.

Let's face it! - English is a crazy language.
> There is no egg in eggplant nor ham in hamburger;
> neither apple nor pine in pineapple.
> English muffins weren't invented in England.
> We take English for granted.

But if we explore its paradoxes,
> we find that quicksand can work slowly,
> boxing rings are square and
> a guinea pig is neither from Guinea nor is it a pig.

And why is it that writers write but

       grocers don't groce and hammers don't ham?

       Doesn't it seem crazy that you can make amends

       but not one amend?

If you have a bunch of odds and ends and

       get rid of all but one of them, what do you call it?

       If teachers taught, why didn't preachers praught?

       If a vegetarian eats vegetables, what does a humanitarian eat?

Sometimes I think all the folks who grew up speaking English

       should be committed to an asylum for the verbally insane.

       In what other language do people recite at a play

       and play at a recital?

       Ship by truck and send cargo by ship?

       Have noses that run and feet that smell?

       How can a slim chance and a fat chance be the same,

       while a wise man and a wise guy are opposites?

You have to marvel at the unique lunacy of a language

       in which your house can burn up as it burns down,

       in which you fill in a form by filling it out and

       in which an alarm goes off by going on.

       If Dad is Pop, how's come Mom isn't Mop?

—Author unknown or anonymous!

Practical Use of Top Down Pronunciation

Practice: Lincoln's Second Inaugural Address
March 4, 1865

Fellow countrymen: / at this **second** appearing / to **take** the **oath** of the **presidential office,** / there is **less** occasion / for an **extended address** / **than there was** at the **first**. / Then a **statement,** / **somewhat** in **detail,** / of a **course** to be **pursued,** / **seemed fitting** and **proper.**

Now, / at the **expiration** of **four years,** / during which **public declarations** have been **constantly called forth** / on **every** point and **phase** / of the **great contest** / which **still** absorbs the **attention** / and **engrosses** the **energies** of the **nation,** / **little** that is **new** / could be **presented.** / The **progress** of our **arms,** / upon which **all else chiefly depends,** / is as **well known** to the **public** / as to **myself;** / and it is, / I **trust,** / **reasonably satisfactory** / and **encouraging** to **all.** / With **high hope** for the **future,** / **no prediction** / in **regard** to it / is **ventured.**

On the **occasion** / **corresponding** to **this** / **four years ago,** / **all thoughts** were **anxiously directed** / to an **impending civil war.** / **All** dreaded it— / **all** sought to **avert it.** / While the **inaugural address** was being **delivered** from this **place,** / **devoted altogether** to **saving** the Union **without** war, / **insurgent agents** were in the **city seeking** to **destroy** it / **without** war— / **seeking** to **dissolve the Union,** / and **divide effects,** / by **negotiation.** / **Both parties deprecated war;** / but one of them / **would make** war / rather than **let** the **nation survive;** / and the **other** would **accept** war / rather than **let** it **perish. And** the **war came.** /

One-eighth of the **whole population** were **colored slaves,** / not **distributed generally** over the **Union,** / but **localized** in the **Southern part** of it. / These **slaves** / **constituted** a **peculiar** / and **powerful interest. /All knew** / that this **interest** was, / **somehow,** / the **cause** of the **war.** / To **strengthen,** / **perpetuate,** / and **extend** this **interest** / was the **object** / for which the **insurgents** / would **rend** the **Union,** / **even** by **war;** / while the **government claimed no right** / to do **more** / than to **restrict** the **territorial enlargement** of it. /

Neither party expected / for the **war** / the **magnitude** / or the **duration** / which it has **already attained**. / **Neither anticipated** / that the <u>cause</u> of the **conflict** might **cease** with, / or **even before,** / the **conflict itself** / should **cease**. / **Each looked** for an **easier triumph,** / and a **result** <u>less</u> **fundamental** / and **astounding**. /

Both read the **same Bible,** / and **pray** to the **same God;** / and <u>each</u> invokes his **aid** / against the **other**. / It may **seem strange** / that **any men should dare** / to **ask** a **just God's assistance** / in **wringing** their **bread** / from the **sweat** of **other men's faces;** / but let us **judge** <u>not</u>, / that we be <u>not judged</u>. / The **prayers** of <u>both</u> could <u>not</u> be answered— / that of <u>neither</u> has been **answered** <u>fully</u>. /

The **Almighty** has his **own purposes**. / "**Woe** unto the **world** / because of **offenses!** / For it **must needs be** / that **offenses come;** / but **woe** to that **man** / by **whom** the **offense cometh**." /

<u>If</u> we shall **suppose** / that **American slavery** is **one** of those **offenses** / which, in the **providence** of **God, must needs come,** / but which, / **having continued** through his **appointed time,** / he <u>now</u> **wills** to **remove,** / and that he **gives** to <u>both</u> **North** and **South** this **terrible war,** / as the <u>woe</u> **due** to those / by whom the **offense came,** / **shall** we **discern** <u>therein</u> any **departure** / from those **divine attributes** / which the **believers** in a **living God** / <u>always</u> ascribe to him? /

Fondly do we **hope—** / **fervently do** we **pray—** / that this **mighty scourge** of **war** / **may speedily pass away**. / **Yet,** / if **God wills** / that it **continue** / until **all** the **wealth** / **piled** by the **bondsman's two hundred** and **fifty years** / of **unrequited toil** shall be **sunk,** / and until **every drop** of **blood** / <u>drawn</u> by the **lash** / shall be **paid** by <u>another</u> / <u>drawn</u> with the **sword,** / as was **said three thousand years ago,** / so **still** it **must be said,** / "The **judgments** of the **Lord** are **true** and **righteous altogether**." /

With **malice** toward **none;** / with **charity** for **all;** / with **firmness** in the **right,** / as **God gives** us to **see** the **right,** / **let us strive** on / to **finish** the **work** we are in; / to **bind up** the **nation's wounds;** / to **care** for him / who shall have **borne** the **battle,** / and for his **widow,** / and his **orphan—** / to **do** <u>all</u> / which may **achieve** and **cherish** / a **just** and **lasting peace** among **ourselves,** / and with **all nations**. /

Vocabulary

Words for pronunciation - *Use backward buildup*

1. **Inaugural:** Opening, or first. Often the first speech as President.
2. **To engross:** To occupy your attention. To absorb.
3. **To venture:** To undertake something a bit dangerous. A new business.
4. **To avert:** To prevent something from happening. To stop. To avoid.
5. **To deprecate:** To criticize. To condemn. To denigrate.
6. **To perish:** To die. To expire. To pass away.
7. **To constitute:** To formally establish something. To found or create.
8. **To perpetuate:** To continue. To make it last, perhaps for generations.
9. **To rend:** To tear. To split apart. To shatter something.
10. **To cease:** To stop.
11. **To dare:** To challenge or taunt someone to do something.
12. **Unrequited:** adj. Unanswered. Not reciprocated.
13. **To toil:** To work really hard. To labor.
14. **To Draw, drawn:** To get. To pull. Drained from.
15. **Malice:** Wish or intent to do harm or hurt.

Related Words

Adjective	Noun	Verb	Adverb
Presidential	President		Presidentially
	Expiration	To expire	
	Invocation	To invoke	
	Offense	To offend	
	Discernment	To discern	
Just	Justice		Justly

—tion Endings

Expiration	Declaration	Prediction
Duration	Invocation	Negotiation

Some Dates

- Lincoln's Election, November 1860
- Seven states left the Union and formed the Confederate States of America before the first Inauguration, March 4, 1861.
- Second Inauguration, March 4, 1865.
- Robert E Lee Surrenders on April 9, 1865. Civil War Ends.
- Lincoln died 42 days after his second inauguration, April 15, 1865.

Questions

- What is the date of this speech?
- What was *The Civil War?*
- Does Lincoln want to predict what will happen with the end of the war?

Past Tense Endings of Regular Verbs

RULE: The letter combination *ed* has three sounds. It usually has the /t/ sound when *ed* is added to words ending in *f, k, p, s, sh, ch,* and *x.* It usually has the /ed/ sound when the base word has the final /t/ or final /d/ sound. When *ed* is added to words ending in other letters, it usually has the /d/ sound.

To extend	Extended /id/	To pursue	Pursued /d/
To present	Presented /id/	To venture	Ventured /d/
To direct	Directed /id/	To Deliver	Delivered /d/
To dread	Dreaded /id/	To destroy	Destroyed /d/
To avert	Averted /id/	To dissolve	Dissolved /d/
To devote	Devoted /id/	To claim	Claimed /d/
To divide	Divided /id/	To judge	Judged /d/
To deprecate	Deprecated /id/	To answer	Answered /d/
To distribute	Distributed /id/	To continue	Continued /d/
To localize	Localized /id/		
To constitute	Constituted /id/	To engross	Engrossed /t/
To anticipate	Anticipated /id/	To cease	Ceased /t/
To perpetuate	Perpetuated /id/	To hope	Hoped /t/
To restrict	Restricted /id/		
To offend	Offended /id/		
To appoint	Appointed /id/		

1. (From Wikipedia) The words "wringing their bread from the sweat of other men's faces" are an allusion to the Fall of Man in the Book of Genesis. As a result of Adam's sin, God tells Adam that henceforth "In the sweat of thy face shalt thou eat bread, till thou return unto the ground; for out of it wast thou taken: for dust thou art, and unto dust shalt thou return" (Gen. 3: 19, KJV).

2. Lincoln's phrase, "but let us judge not, that we be not judged," is an allusion to the words of Jesus in Matthew 7: 1, which in the King James Version reads, "Judge not, that ye be not judged."

3. Lincoln quotes another of Jesus' sayings: "Woe unto the world because of offenses; for it must needs be that offenses come, but woe to that man by whom the offense cometh." Lincoln's quoted language comes from Matthew 18: 7; a similar discourse by Jesus appears in Luke 17: 1.

4. The quotation "the judgments of the Lord are true and righteous altogether" is from Psalm 19: 9 in the King James Bible.

5. The closing paragraph contains two additional glosses from scripture "let us strive on to … bind up the nation's wounds" is a reworking of Psalm 147: 3.[3] Also, "to care for him who shall have borne the battle and for his widow and his orphan" relies on James 1: 27.[4] (Wikipedia)

6. This Inaugural speech takes place near the end of the Civil War. Lincoln is not triumphant, but sad because of the loss of life and the awful cost of the war in terms of people, land and trust in the government.

7. The slaves are near to being freed. In the audience at this time are the assassins, and in the only photo taken of the inauguration, both Lincoln and John Wilkes Booth, his killer can be seen.

Practice: Franklin Delano Roosevelt's First Inaugural Address

(Part one, 212 words)

March 4, 1933

This has been divided into parts to allow time for vocabulary and comprehension of the content without making individual practices too long. After all parts have been completed, the entire speech is repeated as a single practice to be repeated for several days in order to build stamina.

President Hoover, ⟍/ **Mr. Chief Justice,** ⟍/ my friends: ⟍/ This is a day of national consecration. / **And** / I am **certain** / that on this **day** / my **fellow Americans expect** / that on my **induction** into the **Presidency,** / I will **address** them / with a **candor** / and a **decision** / which the **present situation** of our **people impels.** / This is **preeminently** / the **time** to **speak** the **truth,** / the **whole truth,** / **frankly** and **boldly.** / **Nor need** we **shrink** / from **honestly facing conditions** / in our **country today.** / This **great Nation** will **endure,** / as it has **endured,** / will **revive** and will **prosper.** ⟍

So, / **first** of **all,** / **let** me **assert** my **firm belief** / that the **only thing** we have to **fear** / is **fear itself** — **nameless,** / **unreasoning,** / **unjustified terror** / which **paralyzes needed efforts** / to **convert retreat** into **advance.** / In **every dark hour** / of our **national life,** / a **leadership** of **frankness** / and of **vigor**/ has **met** with that **understanding** / and **support** of the **people themselves** / which is **essential** to **victory.** / And I am **convinced** / that you will **again** / **give** that **support** to **leadership** in these **critical days.** ⟍

Vocabulary

1. **Consecration:** The action of making something sacred. The presidency is a sacred leadership position in the USA.

2. **Induction:** Formally bringing someone into a position or job of trust and honor.

3. **Candor.** Open honesty.

4. **Impels:** Forces me. Urges me. Drives me. Makes me want to do something.

5. **Preeminently:** Above all. First and foremost.

6. **Shrink, shrank, shrunk:** To become smaller. To move away because of fear.

7. **Endure:** Suffer through something difficult or painful. Hopefully enduring will make a person learn and be the better for it.

8. **Revive:** Give new strength. Improve the condition of something or someone.

9. **Prosper:** Succeed in material ways. God has prospered our nation.

10. **Assert:** Say something confidently and forcefully.

11. **Unjustified:** Something not reasonable or right.

12. **Paralyzes:** Causes a person to become unable to move. Bring a system to a stop.

13. **Convert retreat into advance:** Go forward and stop going backward.

14. **Frankness:** Open honesty. Telling the truth.

15. **Vigor:** Strength. Effort. Enthusiasm.

16. **Essential:** Critical. Important. Necessary.

17. **Victory:** An act of winning in a contest, election, or war.

Franklin Delano Roosevelt's First Inaugural Address (Part 2, 347 words)

In such a **spirit** / on **my part** and on **yours** / we **face our common difficulties.** / They **concern,** / **thank God,** / **only material things.** / **Values** have **shrunk** to **fantastic levels;** / **taxes** have **risen;** / **our ability** to **pay** has **fallen;** / **government** of **all kinds** / is **faced** by **serious curtailment** of **income;** / the **means** of **exchange** are **frozen** in the **currents of trade;** / the **withered leaves** of **industrial enterprise** / **lie** on **every side;** / **farmers find no markets** for their **produce;** / and the **savings** of **many years** / in **thousands** of **families** are **gone.** / **More important,** / a **host** of **unemployed citizens** / **face** the **grim problem** of **existence,** / and an **equally great number toil** with **little return.** / **Only** a **foolish optimist** / can **deny** the **dark realities** of the **moment.**

And yet / our **distress comes** from **no failure** of **substance.** / We are **stricken** by **no plague** of **locusts.** / **Compared** with the **perils** / which our **forefathers conquered,** / because they **believed** and were **not afraid,** / we **have still much** to be **thankful for.** / **Nature** still **offers** her **bounty** / and **human efforts** have **multiplied** it. / **Plenty** is at our **doorstep,** / but a **generous use** of it / **languishes** in the **very sight** of the **supply.**

Primarily, / this is because the **rulers** / of the **exchange of mankind's goods** / **have failed,** / through their **own stubbornness** / and their **own incompetence,** / have **admitted their failure,** / and have **abdicated.** / **Practices** of the **unscrupulous moneychangers** / **stand indicted** / in the **court** of **public opinion,** / **rejected** by the **hearts** and **minds of men.**

True, / they have **tried.** / **But their efforts** have been **cast** / in the **pattern** of an **outworn tradition.** / **Faced** by **failure** of **credit,** / they have **proposed** only the **lending of more money.** / **Stripped** of the **lure** of **profit** / by which to **induce our people** / to **follow** their **false leadership,** / they have **resorted** to **exhortations,** / **pleading tearfully** for **restored confidence.** / They **only know** the **rules** of a **generation** of **self-seekers.** / **They have no vision,** / and when there is **no vision** the **people perish.**

Vocabulary

1. **Material things:** Anything that man has made ranging from necessities to luxury items. It can go from a comb to a yacht.

2. **Fantastic:** Unbelievable.

3. **Curtailment:** The action or fact of reducing or restricting something.

4. **Means of exchange:** Money in any form. Coins, Stocks, Loans, Bartering.

5. **Withered:** Dried and dead. No longer prosperous or working well. *The withered leaves of industrial enterprise means that the companies and business, even farming, no longer produces or works.*

6. **The grim problem of existence:** No house, or shelter or food. Starvation and homelessness.

7. **Equally great number toil with little return:** Means to work hard for little money. Can barely make enough money to eat.

8. **To languish:** Grow weak. Fail to be successful.

9. **The rulers / of the exchange of mankind's goods / have failed:** Means poor and greedy leadership in political and financial power have failed.

10. **Abdicated:** Failed to undertake the responsibility of the job both politically and financially (Banks and stock market.)

11. **Unscrupulous:** Those with no morals or sense of fairness.

12. **Indicted:** Formally accused of a serious crime. Indicted for fraud, murder, manslaughter, robbery.

13. **Lure:** Temptation or the strong quality of money, a better job, etc.

14. **Stripped:** Reduced or removed. No longer possess something.

15. **Induce:** Try to persuade people to follow their false leadership.

16. **Exhortations:** Address emphatically urging someone. *(Vote for me; Follow me; This is best for you!)*

Franklin Delano Roosevelt's First Inaugural Address (Part 3, 294 words)

Yes, / the **money changers** have **fled** / from their **high seats** / in the **temple** of our **civilization**. / We may **now restore** that **temple** / to the **ancient truths**. / The **measure** of that **restoration** / **lies** in the **extent** / to which we **apply social values more noble** / than **mere monetary profit**.

Happiness lies not in the **mere possession** of **money**; / it **lies** in the **joy** of **achievement**, / in the **thrill** of **creative effort**. / The **joy**, / the **moral stimulation** of **work** / **no longer must be forgotten**/ in the **mad chase** of **evanescent profits**. / These **dark days**, / my **friends**, / will be **worth all** they **cost us** / if they **teach us** / that **our true destiny** / is **not** to be **ministered** <u>unto</u> / but to **minister** to **ourselves**, / to **our fellow men**.

Recognition / of that **falsity** of **material wealth** / as the **standard** of **success** / **goes hand** in **hand** with the **abandonment** / of the **false belief** / that **public office** / and **high political position** / are to be **valued** <u>only</u> by the **standards** / of **pride** of **place** and **personal profit**; / and there must be an **end** / to a **conduct** in **banking** and in **business** / which **too often** has **given** to a **sacred trust** / the **likeness** of **callous** / and **selfish wrongdoing**. / **Small wonder** / that **confidence languishes**, / for it **thrives** <u>only</u> on **honesty**, / on **honor**, / on the **sacredness** of **obligations**, / on **faithful protection**, / and on **unselfish performance**; / without them / it **cannot live**.

Restoration calls, / however, / **not** for **changes** in **ethics alone**. / This **Nation** is **asking** for **action**, / and **action now**.

Vocabulary

1. **Money Changers:** Bankers and Wall Street Stock Market. The market crashed in 1929 and the banks failed. The Great Depression took place. In 1933, the people suffered.

2. **Noble:** Higher qualities of human rights and methods of helping.

3. **Evanescent:** Disappearing. Soon passing out of sight. A beautiful bubble gone in a minute.

4. **To minister:** To help others. To attend to the needs of others.

5. **Abandonment:** Leaving of stop supporting. The action of abandoning.

6. **Callous:** Insensitive and cruel disregard for others.

7. **Languishes:** Grows weak or feeble. Lacks energy and vitality.

8. **Obligations:** Morally and legally bound to do something. *A father has many obligations to his wife and children.*

9. **Restoration:** To bring something back in form or custom. To return something.

Franklin Delano Roosevelt's First Inaugural Address (Part 4, 321 words)

Our greatest primary task / is to **put people** to **work.** / This is **no unsolvable problem** / if we **face** it **wisely** and **courageously.** / It can be **accomplished** in **part** / by **direct recruiting** by the **Government itself,** / **treating** the **task** / as we would **treat** the **emergency** of a **war,** / but at the **same time,** / through this **employment,** / **accomplishing great—** / **greatly needed projects** / to **stimulate** and **reorganize** / the **use** of our **great natural resources.**

Hand in hand with that / we **must** <u>**frankly**</u> **recognize** / the **overbalance** of **population** / in our **industrial centers** / **and,** / by **engaging** on a **national scale** / in a **redistribution,** / <u>**endeavor**</u> to **provide** a **better use** of the **land** / for those **best fitted** for the **land.**

Yes, / the **task** can be **helped** by **definite efforts** / to **raise** the **values** of **agricultural products,** / and with this the **power** to **purchase** / the **output** of our **cities.** / It can be **helped** / by **preventing realistically** / the **tragedy** of the **growing loss** / through **foreclosure** / of our **small homes** and our **farms.**

It can be **helped** by **insistence** / that the **Federal,** / the **State,** / and the **local governments** / **act forthwith** on the **demand** /that their **cost be drastically reduced.**

It can be **helped** / by the **unifying** of **relief activities** / which **today** are **often scattered,** / **uneconomical,** / **unequal.**

It can be **helped** / by **national planning** <u>**for**</u> / and **supervision** <u>**of**</u> / **all forms** of **transportation** / and of **communications** / and **other utilities** / that have a **definitely public character.**

There are **many ways** in which it can be **helped,** /
but it can <u>**never**</u> be **helped** / by <u>**merely**</u> **talking** about it.

We must act. / **We must act quickly.**

And **finally,** / in our **progress towards** a **resumption** of **work,** / we **require two safeguards** / against a **return** of the **evils** / of the **old order.** / There **must** be a **strict supervision** / of **all banking** / and **credits** / and **investments.** / There **must** be an **end** / to **speculation** with **other people's money.** / And there **must** be **provision** / for an **adequate** / but **sound currency.**

Vocabulary

1. **Stimulate:** Encourage great interest and activity.

2. **Endeavor:** Try really hard to achieve something.

3. **Foreclosure:** the act of taking possession of a property when the payments are not made. *A house or a car can be foreclosed or repossessed by the bank.*

4. **Drastically:** Doing something in a way that has a strong and far-reaching effect.

5. **Scattered:** Throw something in random directions.

6. **Utilities:** A public utility like a service provide. The water and sewer department is a public utility.

7. **Merely:** Only. Simply. Solely.

8. **Resumption:** The action of beginning something again.

Franklin Delano Roosevelt's First Inaugural Address (Part 5, 291 words)

These, my **friends,** / are the **lines** of **attack.** / I shall **presently urge** / upon a **new Congress** in **special session/ detailed measures** / for their **fulfillment,** / and I shall **seek** / the **immediate assistance** of the **48 States.**

Through this **program** of **action** / we **address ourselves** / to **putting our own national house** in **order** / and **making income** / **balance outgo.** / Our **international trade relations,** / though **vastly important,** / are in **point** of **time,** / and **necessity,** / **secondary** to the **establishment** / of a **sound national economy.** / I **favor,** / as a **practical policy,** / the **putting** of **first things first.** /

I shall **spare no effort** / to **restore world trade** by **international economic readjustment;** / but the **emergency** at **home** / **cannot wait** on that **accomplishment.**

The **basic thought** / that **guides these specific means** of **national recovery** / is **not nationally** — / **narrowly nationalistic.** / It is the **insistence,** as a **first consideration,** / upon the **interdependence** of the **various elements** / in and **parts** / of the **United States** of **America** —/ a **recognition** of the **old** / and **permanently important manifestation** / of the **American spirit** of the **pioneer.** / It is the **way** to **recovery.** / It is the **immediate way.** / It is the **strongest assurance** / that **recovery** will **endure.**

In the **field** of **world policy,** / I would **dedicate** this **Nation** / to the **policy** of the **good neighbor:** / the **neighbor** who **resolutely respects himself** / and, / because he **does so,** / **respects** the **rights of others;** / the **neighbor** who **respects** his **obligations** / and **respects** the **sanctity** / of his **agreements** in and with a **world** of **neighbors.**

Vocabulary

1. **Urge:** (verb) try earnestly or persistently to persuade (someone) to do something.

2. **Urge:** (noun) a strong desire or impulse.

3. **Vastly:** to a very great extent; immensely.

4. **Immediate [uh med dee ʸut]:** occurring or done at once; instant.

5. **A sound economy:** The careful use of money, resources, and means of production.

6. **Spare no effort:** Do everything one possibly can in order to achieve something.

7. **Readjustment:** Adapting to a changed situation.

8. **Manifestation:** An event that clearly shows something. A returning of the old working pioneer spirit.

9. **The recovery:** A return to a strong country current caught in the Great Depression.

10. **Obligations:** Duty. What one is morally and legally bound to do.

11. **Sanctity:** Sacred. The trust of a Treaty or boundaries of a country.

Franklin Delano Roosevelt's First Inaugural Address (Part 6, 397 words)

If I **read** the **temper** of our **people correctly,** / we **now realize,** / as we have **never realized before,** / our **interdependence** on **each other;** / that we can **not merely take,** / but we must **give as well;** / that if we are to **go forward,** / we must **move** / as a **trained** and **loyal army** / **willing** to **sacrifice** for the **good** / of a **common discipline,** / because without **such discipline** / **no progress** can be **made,** / **no leadership becomes effective.**

We are, I **know,** / **ready** and **willing** to **submit** our **lives** / and our **property** to **such discipline,** / because it **makes possible** a **leadership** / which **aims** at the **larger good.** / **This,** / **I propose** to **offer,** / **pledging** that the **larger purposes** will **bind** upon us, / **bind** upon us **all** / as a **sacred obligation** / with a **unity** of **duty** **hitherto evoked** / **only** in **times** of **armed strife.**

With this **pledge taken,** / I **assume unhesitatingly** the **leadership** of this **great army** of our **people** / **dedicated** to a **disciplined attack** / **upon our common problems.**

Action in this **image,** / **action** to this **end** is **feasible** / under the **form** of **government** / which we have **inherited** from our **ancestors.**

Our Constitution is **so simple,** / **so practical** / that it is **possible always** / to **meet extraordinary needs** / by **changes** in **emphasis** and **arrangement** / without **loss** of **essential form.** / That is why **our constitutional system** has **proved itself** / the **most superbly enduring political mechanism** / the **modern world** has **ever seen.**

It has **met every stress** / of **vast expansion** of **territory,** / of **foreign wars,** / of **bitter internal strife,** / of **world relations.** / And it is to be **hoped** / that the **normal balance** of **executive** / and **legislative authority** / may be **wholly equal,** / **wholly adequate** / to **meet** the **unprecedented task** before us. / But it may be / that an **unprecedented demand** / and **need** for **undelayed action** / may **call** for **temporary departure** / from that **normal balance** of **public procedure.**

I am **prepared** / under my **constitutional duty** / to **recommend** the **measures** / that a **stricken nation** / in the **midst** of a **stricken world** / may **require.** / These **measures,** / or **such other measures** / as the **Congress** may **build** / **out** of its **experience** and **wisdom,** / I shall **seek,** / within my **constitutional authority,** / to **bring** to **speedy adoption.**

Vocabulary

1. **The temper of our people:** The state of mind of the Americans. What Americans need and want now to help them in the Great Depression. The people are hungry, jobless, the banks have failed, and the situation is bad.

2. **Bind upon us:** Come together for a greater cause.

3. **Hitherto evoked:** Until now, or until the time in discussion; It is now brought to the conscious mind. *Before, we only had to sacrifice like this during a war.*

4. **Feasible:** Possible to do easily and conveniently.

5. **Ancestors:** A person earlier than a grandparent from whom you are descended.

6. **Unprecedented:** Never done before or never known of before this time.

7. **Stricken:** Seriously affected by an undesirable condition, like a serious illness or financial disaster.

Franklin Delano Roosevelt's First Inaugural Address (Part 7, 297 words)

But, / in the **event** / that the **Congress** shall **fail** to **take one** of these **two courses,** / in the **event** / that the **national emergency** is **still critical,** / I shall **not evade** the **clear course** of **duty** / that will then **confront** me. / I shall **ask** the **Congress** / for the **one remaining instrument** to **meet** the **crisis** — / **broad Executive power** / to **wage** a **war** against the **emergency,** / as **great** as the **power** / that would be **given** to me / if we were in **fact invaded** by a **foreign foe.** / For the **trust reposed** in me, / I will **return** the **courage** / and the **devotion** / that **befit** the **time.** / I can **do no less.**

We **face** the **arduous days** / that **lie** before us / in the **warm courage** of **national unity;** / with the **clear consciousness** / of **seeking old** and **precious moral values;** / with the **clean satisfaction** / that **comes** from the **stern performance** of **duty** / by **old** and **young alike.** / We **aim** at the **assurance** / of a **rounded,** / a **permanent national life.**

We **do not distrust** the — / the **future** of **essential democracy.** / The **people** of the **United States** have **not failed.** / In their **need** / they have **registered** a **mandate** / that they **want direct,** / **vigorous action.** / They have **asked** for **discipline** / and **direction** under **leadership.** / They have **made** me the **present instrument** / of their **wishes.** In the **spirit** of the **gift** I **take it.**

In this **dedication** — / In this **dedication** of a **Nation, we humbly ask** the **blessing** of **God.**

May He protect each and **every one of us.**

May He guide me in the **days** to **come.**

Vocabulary

1. **Critical:** A crisis. A problem that can become disastrous. *The situation in the USA was critical when President Roosevelt was inaugurated.*

2. **Not evade:** Not avoid or deny the situation.

3. **Reposed:** Given or placed in the President.

5. **Arduous:** Difficult and tiring. Something that requires great effort and work.

6. **Mandate:** An official order to do something. The authority to carry out the policy and the power of the Presidency.

Franklin Delano Roosevelt's First Inaugural Address (in its entirety)

In total, the speech contains 1,933 Words. At the normal rate of 150 wpm it should take about 13 minutes to speak. Emphasis and pauses, can add an extra 5 minutes, so the speech should still be less than 20 minutes. This is good practice for stamina, clarity, intelligibility, rate of speaking, power English and all the steps presented in this book.

Read the entire speech in a single session. Do this once a day for several days in a row.

President Hoover, ↘/ Mr. Chief Justice, ↘/ my friends: ↘/ This is a day of national consecration. / And / I am certain / that on this day / my fellow Americans expect / that on my induction into the Presidency, / I will address them / with a candor / and a decision / which the present situation of our people impels. / This is preeminently / the time to speak the truth, / the whole truth, / frankly and boldly. / Nor need we shrink / from honestly facing conditions / in our country today. / This great Nation will endure, / as it has endured, / will revive and will prosper. ↘

So, / first of all, / let me assert my firm belief / that the only thing we have to fear / is fear itself — nameless, / unreasoning, / unjustified terror / which paralyzes needed efforts / to convert retreat into advance. / In every dark hour / of our national life, / a leadership of frankness / and of vigor/ has met with that understanding / and support of the people themselves / which is essential to victory. / And I am convinced / that you will again / give that support to leadership in these critical days. ↘

In such a **spirit** / on **my part** and on **yours** / we **face our common difficulties.** / They **concern,** / **thank God,** / **only material things.** / **Values** have **shrunk** to **fantastic levels;** / **taxes** have **risen;** / **our ability** to **pay** has **fallen;** / **government** of **all kinds** / is **faced** by **serious curtailment of income;** / the **means of exchange** are **frozen** in the **currents of trade;** / the **withered leaves** of **industrial enterprise** / **lie** on **every side;** / **farmers find no markets** for their **produce;** / and the **savings of many years** / in **thousands of families** are **gone.** / **More important,** / a **host** of **unemployed citizens** / **face** the **grim problem** of existence, / and an **equally great number toil** with **little return.** / **Only** a **foolish optimist** / can **deny** the **dark realities** of th**e moment.**

And yet / **our distress comes** from **no failure** of **substance.** / We are **stricken** by **no plague** of **locusts.** / **Compared** with the **perils** / which our **forefathers conquered,** / because they **believed** and were **not afraid,** / we **have still much** to be **thankful for.** / **Nature** <u>still</u> **offers** her **bounty** / and **human efforts** have **multiplied** it. / **Plenty** is at our **doorstep,** / but a **generous use** of it / **languishes** in the **very sight** of the **supply.**

Primarily, / this is because the **rulers** / of the **exchange** of **mankind's goods** / **have failed,** / through their **own stubbornness** / and their **own incompetence,** / have **admitted their failure,** / and have **abdicated.** / **Practices** of the **unscrupulous moneychangers** / **stand indicted** / in the **court** of **public opinion,** / **rejected** by the **hearts** and **minds** of **men.**

True, / they have **tried.** / **But their efforts** have been **cast** / in the **pattern** of an **outworn tradition.** / **Faced** by **failure** of **credit,** / they have **proposed** <u>only</u> the **lending** of **more money.** / **Stripped** of the **lure** of **profit** / by which to **induce our people** / to **follow** their **false leadership,** / they have **resorted** to **exhortations,** / **pleading tearfully** for **restored confidence.** / They **only know** the **rules** of a **generation** of **self-seekers.** / **They have no vision,** / and when there is **no vision** the **people perish.**

Yes, / the **money changers** have **fled** / from their **high seats** / in the **temple** of our **civilization.** / We may **now restore** that **temple** / to the **ancient truths.** / The **measure** of that **restoration** / **lies** in the **extent** / to which we **apply social values more noble** / than **mere monetary profit.**

Happiness lies not in the **mere possession of money;** / it **lies** in the **joy** of **achievement,** / in the **thrill** of **creative effort.** / The **joy,** / the **moral stimulation** of **work** / **no longer must be forgotten**/ in the **mad chase** of **evanescent profits.** / These **dark days,** / my **friends,** / will be **worth all** they **cost us** / if they **teach us** / that **our true destiny** / is **not** to be **ministered** <u>unto</u> / but to **minister** to **ourselves,** / to **our fellow men.**

Recognition / of that **falsity** of **material wealth** / as the **standard** of **success** / goes **hand** in **hand** with the **abandonment** / of the **false belief** / that **public office**

/ and **high political position** / are to be **valued only** by the **standards** / of **pride** of **place** and **personal profit;** / and there must be an **end** / to a **conduct** in **banking** and in **business** / which **too often** has **given** to a **sacred trust** / the **likeness** of **callous** / and **selfish wrongdoing.** / **Small wonder** / that **confidence languishes,** / for it **thrives only** on **honesty,** / on **honor,** / on the **sacredness** of **obligations,** / on **faithful protection,** / and on **unselfish performance;** / without them / it **cannot live.**

Restoration calls, / however, / **not** for **changes** in **ethics alone.** / This **Nation** is **asking** for **action,** / and **action now.**

Our greatest primary task / is to **put people** to **work.** / This is **no unsolvable problem** / if we **face** it **wisely** and **courageously.** / It can be **accomplished** in **part** / by **direct recruiting** by the **Government itself,** / **treating** the **task** / as we would **treat** the **emergency** of a **war,** / but at the **same time,** / through this **employment,** / **accomplishing great—** / **greatly needed projects** / to **stimulate** and **reorganize** / the **use** of our **great natural resources.**

Hand in **hand** with that / we **must frankly recognize** / the **overbalance** of **population** / in our **industrial centers** / **and,** / by **engaging** on a **national scale** / in a **redistribution,** / **endeavor** to **provide** a **better use** of the **land** / for those **best fitted** for the **land.**

Yes, / the **task** can be **helped** by **definite efforts** / to **raise** the **values** of **agricultural products,** / and with this the **power** to **purchase** / the **output** of our **cities.** / It can be **helped** / by **preventing realistically** / the **tragedy** of the **growing loss** / through **foreclosure** / of our **small homes** and our **farms.**

It can be **helped** by **insistence** / that the **Federal,** / the **State,** / and the **local governments** / **act forthwith** on the **demand** /that their **cost be drastically reduced.**

It can be **helped** / by the **unifying** of **relief activities** / which **today** are **often scattered,** / **uneconomical,** / **unequal.**

It can be **helped** / by **national planning for** / and **supervision of** / **all forms** of **transportation** / and of **communications** / and **other utilities** / that have a **definitely public character.**

There are **many ways** in which it can be **helped, /**
but it can **never** be helped / by **merely talking** about it.

We must act. / We must act quickly.

And **finally,** / in our **progress towards** a **resumption** of **work,** / we **require two safeguards** / against a **return** of the **evils** / of the **old order.** / There **must** be a **strict supervision** / of **all banking** / and **credits** / and **investments.** / There **must** be an **end** / to **speculation** with **other people's money.** / And there **must** be **provision** / for an **adequate** / **but sound currency.**

These, my **friends,** / are the **lines** of **attack.** / I shall **presently urge** / upon a **new Congress** in **special session/ detailed measures** / for their **fulfillment,** / and I shall **seek** / the **immediate assistance** of the **48 States.**

Through this **program** of **action** / we **address ourselves** / to **putting our own national house** in **order** / and **making income** / **balance outgo.** / Our **international trade relations,** / though **vastly important,** / are in **point** of **time,** / and **necessity,** / **secondary** to the **establishment** / of a **sound national economy.** / I **favor,** / as a **practical policy,** / the **putting** of **first things first.** /

I shall **spare no effort** / to **restore world trade** by **international economic readjustment;** / but the **emergency** at **home** / **cannot wait** on that **accomplishment.**

The **basic thought** / that **guides these specific means** of **national recovery** / is **not nationally —** / **narrowly nationalistic.** / It is the **insistence,** as a **first consideration,** / upon the **interdependence** of the **various elements** / in and **parts** / of the **United States** of **America —**/ a **recognition** of the **old** / and **permanently important manifestation** / of the **American spirit** of the **pioneer.** / It is the **way** to **recovery.** / It is the **immediate way.** / It is the **strongest assurance** / that **recovery** will **endure.**

In the **field** of **world policy,** / I would **dedicate** this **Nation** / to the **policy** of the **good neighbor:** / the **neighbor** who **resolutely respects himself** / and, / because he **does so,** / **respects** the **rights** of **others;** / the **neighbor** who **respects** his **obligations** / and **respects** the **sanctity** / of his **agreements** in and with a **world** of **neighbors.**

If I **read** the **temper** of our **people correctly,** / we **now realize,** / as we have **never realized before,** / our **interdependence** on **each other;** / that we can **not merely take,** / but we must **give as well;** / that if we are to **go forward,** / we must **move** / as a **trained** and **loyal army** / **willing** to **sacrifice** for the **good** / of a **common discipline,** / because without **such discipline** / **no progress** can be **made,** / **no leadership becomes effective.**

We are, I **know,** / **ready** and **willing** to **submit** our **lives** / and our **property** to **such discipline,** / because it **makes possible** a **leadership** / which **aims** at the **larger good.** / **This,** / **I propose** to **offer,** / **pledging** that the **larger purposes** will **bind** upon us, / **bind** upon us **all** / as a **sacred obligation** / with a **unity** of **duty hitherto evoked** / only in **times** of **armed strife.**

With this **pledge taken,** / I **assume unhesitatingly** the **leadership** of this **great army** of our **people** / **dedicated** to a **disciplined attack** / **upon our common problems.**

Action in this **image,** / **action** to this **end** is **feasible** / under the **form** of **government** / which we have **inherited** from our **ancestors.**

Our Constitution is **so simple,** / **so practical** / that it is **possible always** / to **meet extraordinary needs** / by **changes** in **emphasis** and **arrangement** / without **loss** of **essential form.** / That is why **our constitutional system** has **proved itself** / the **most superbly enduring political mechanism** / the **modern world** has **ever seen.**

It has **met every stress** / of **vast expansion** of **territory,** / of **foreign wars,** / of **bitter internal strife,** / of **world relations.** / And it is to be **hoped** / that the **normal balance** of **executive** / and **legislative authority** / may be **wholly equal,** / **wholly adequate** / to **meet** the **unprecedented task** before us. / But it may be / that an **unprecedented demand** / and **need** for **undelayed action** / may **call** for **temporary departure** / from that **normal balance** of **public procedure.**

I am **prepared** / under my **constitutional duty** / to **recommend** the **measures** / that a **stricken nation** / in the **midst** of a **stricken world** / may **require.** / These **measures,** / or **such other measures** / as the **Congress** may **build** / **out** of its **experience** and **wisdom,** / I shall **seek,** / within my **constitutional authority,** / to **bring** to **speedy adoption.**

But, / in the **event** / that the **Congress** shall **fail** to **take one** of these **two courses,** / in the **event** / that the **national emergency** is **still critical,** / I shall **not evade** the **clear course** of **duty** / that will then **confront** me. / I shall **ask** the **Congress** / for the **one remaining instrument** to **meet** the **crisis** — / **broad Executive power** / to **wage** a **war** against the **emergency,** / as **great** as the **power** / that would be **given** to me / if we were in **fact invaded** by a **foreign foe.** / For the **trust reposed** in me, / I will **return** the **courage** / and the **devotion** / that **befit** the **time.** / I can **do no less.**

We **face** the **arduous days** / that **lie** before us / in the **warm courage** of **national unity;** / with the **clear consciousness** / of **seeking old** and **precious moral values;** / with the **clean satisfaction** / that **comes** from the **stern performance** of **duty** / by **old** and **young alike.** / We **aim** at the **assurance** / of a **rounded,** / a **permanent national life.**

We **do not distrust** the — / the **future** of **essential democracy.** / The **people** of the **United States** have **not failed.** / In their **need** / they have **registered** a **mandate** / that they **want direct,** / **vigorous action.** / They have **asked** for **discipline** / and **direction** under **leadership.** / They have **made** me the **present instrument** / of their **wishes.** In the **spirit** of the **gift** I **take it.**

In this dedication — / In this **dedication** of a **Nation, we humbly ask** the **blessing** of **God.**

May He protect each and **every one of us.**

May He guide me in the **days** to **come.**

APPENDIX

Spanish / English Sounds

There are a few significant sounds in English that differ only slightly from Spanish. The Spanish student will naturally try to substitute the Spanish sounds for English sounds whose articulation is similar to Spanish sounds.

Working with Minimal Pairs

The sounds mentioned below are some of the most common problems we find when Spanish-speaking people use English.

The *day/they* problem: the voiced /th/ sound is replaced with a /d/ sound.

than —> dan	those —> doze	other—> udder
breathing —> breeding	father —> fodder	lather —> ladder

The sin/thin problem: the UN-voiced /th/ sound is replaced with a /s/ sound such that "thank" becomes "sank."

thigh —> sigh	thought —> sought	thicker —> sicker
thumb —> some	bath —> bass	forth —> force

The ship/chip problem: the /sh/ is pronounced like a /ch/, so a word like "share" is pronounced "chair."

cheat —> sheet	cherry —> sherry	watches —> washes
matched —> mashed	chew —> shoe	crutch —> crush

The van/ ban problem: both /b/ and /v/ are pronounced as a /b/. Therefore, a word like "vat" is pronounced like "bat."

veep —> beep	volt —> bolt	very —> berry
curved —>curbed	loaves —> lobes	prevent —> prebent

The rag/ rack problem: the /k/ sound in the final position has a /g/ sound. Thus, a word like "rack" is pronounced like "rag."

sag —> sack	stag —> stack	crag —> crack

The tin/ den problem: the /t/ in the initial position is pronounced like a /d/. So, "tad" becomes "dad."

tally —> dally	ton —> done	tell —> dell
tried —> dried	slighting —> sliding	bet —> bed
town —> down	trip —> drip	at —> add

The zinc/ sink problem: the /z/ sound is pronounced like the unvoiced /s/ sound. So, "buzz" becomes "bus."

seal —> zeal	sip —> zip	sift —> shift
sue —> zoo	place —> plays	lice —> lies
dense —> dens	since —> sins	sing —> zing

The jello/ yellow problem: the /j/ sound is pronounced like a /y/. So the word "jealous" becomes "yellous" which is not a word in English. The /j/ sound is voiced. The /y/ sound is unvoiced.

gyp —> yip	jeer —> year	jam —> yam
hedge —> hay	fridge —> free	jet —> yet
jack —> yak	jail —> Yale	joke —> yolk

The pull/pool problem: the /u/ (up) is pronounced like /uw / (ooop), so a word like "pull" is pronounced like "pool."

look —> Luke	full —> fool	good —> gooed
hood —> who'd	stood —> stewed	would —> wooed

The still/ steel problem: the /i/(short I) is pronounced like /e/ (long eeee), so "fill" is pronounced like "feel." This brings in the "sheet," "beach," and all other long e problem words for the Spanish speakers.

bead —> bid	leased —> list	peel —> pill
feet —> fit	kneel —> nil	team —> tim

Above "Spanish / English Sounds" was adapted from *Lessons in English Pronunciation for Spanish Speakers.* Dept. of HEW. Washington, DC, and from *Pronunciation Contrasts in English* by Nilsen and Nilsen

Common Asian Language Interference Sound Changes

(Much of this material was presented at an International TESOL meeting in 1979.)

Chinese, Korean, Japanese, Vietnamese and other Asian languages have sound changes that interfere with proper pronunciation of English. These changes often occur between two words. The six or seven stops in English are the t, d, p, k, g, an j and sometimes b. The nasal sounds are m and n.

With Language Interference, if a stop (such as a t) is followed by a nasal (such as an m) the stop can be changed to sound like a nasal. Here are some examples:

t+m becomes n+m	"meet me" becomes "meen me"
b+n becomes m+n	"club news" becomes "clum news"
t+n becomes n+n	"at night" becomes "an night"

The /l/ with /n/, /r/ and /m/ problem:

l+n becomes l+l	"all night" becomes "all light"
n+l becomes l+l	"ten lamps" becomes "tel lamps"
l+r becomes l+l	"all right" becomes "all light"
m+l becomes m+n	"some light" becomes "some night"

The /t/ and /d/ problem found with *you* or *your*

t+y becomes n+y	"what you" [whatchew] becomes "whan you"
d+y becomes d+n	"did you" [didjew] becomes "din you"

Practice: Hard Sound Changes

Up many	At most	Back me ʸup	Keep now
That never	Picnic	Rob me	Sad movie
Big map	Hobnailed	Bad night	Stagnant
But now	Take me ʸout		

We walked up many stairs.

There were only thirty at most.

Please back me up [back meʸup] at the meeting.

This one we can keep now.

That never should have been said.

I like a good picnic.

That guy plans to rob me.

It was a very sad movie.

He showed us a big map.

He wore hobnailed boots.

He had a bad night and didn't sleep well.

The pond held stagnant water.

He was sick but now he's okay.

Take me out to the ball game.

Practice: *p* Between Two Vowels

open	repose	a pet	a pair	apart
Tipping	whipping	ripping	shipping	
Pepper	apple	happen	puppet	Copper
Cooper	three parts	three pets	two pots	
three parks	a piece of pie			

Practice: The /f/ and /p/ Exercise

Contrast the /p/ and /f/ problem. For many Asians, the /p/ and the / f/ sound the same. Think of the Spanish /b/ and /v/ or the /r/ and /l/ that sound the same.

> a pair becomes affair
> snipping becomes sniffing
> two pans becomes two fans
> new pace becomes new face
> real pact becomes real fact
> appear becomes a fear

Practice these /f/ and /p/ word pairs

> I bought two new pans.
> I bought two new fans.
>
> Ours is a real pact.
> Ours is a real fact.
>
> I need a cup of that.
> I need a cuff of that.
>
> She made a sheep out of paper.
> She made a sheaf of paper.
>
> We saw a clip in that picture.
> We saw a cliff in that picture.

The problems with R and L

The letters l and r are actually the same in Korean, Japanese, Chinese and other Asian languages.

This sound sometimes sounds like /r/ and sometimes like /l/ to English speakers. It even can sound like /d/ to Americans.

Practice sentences with L contrasted with N and D.

No. My <u>dough</u> is <u>low</u>.

Do you <u>know</u> <u>Lou</u>?

Every <u>day</u> the hen will <u>lay</u>.

A <u>"D"</u> is the grade that <u>Lee</u> got.

At <u>night</u> there is no <u>light</u>.

My <u>debt</u> is high; <u>let</u> me pay it over 5 years.

Final L: An L at the end of a syllable is a bit different from one at the beginning.

mill	bell	tell	ill	chill	mail
pal	gal	doll	ball	tall	mole
till	toll	duel	dull	mile	bowl

An L before a final consonant sound can be like /U/

milk	film	silk	ilk	elk	pulp
sulk	help	dolphin	squelch	all's well	

An L before /t, d/ sound is pronounced strongly.

belt	held	melt	called	cold

It is usually not necessary to pronounce the /l/ at all after a back vowel (unless the /l/ is followed by a /t/ or /d/. It becomes a silent /l/.

talk	walk	folk	yolk	caulk
calm	balm	palm	chalk	

Practice: The Bells, By Edgar Allen Poe

Hear the sledges with the bells ...
    Silver bells!
    What a world of merriment their melody foretells!

How they tinkle, tinkle, tinkle,
    In the icy air of night!
    While the stars that oversprinkle
    All the heavens, seem to twinkle
    With a crystalline delight;

Keeping time, time, time,
    In a sort of Runic rhyme,
    To the tintinnabulation that so musically wells
    From the bells, bells, bells, bells,
    Bells, bells, bells...
    From the jingling and the tinkling of the bells,

Hear the mellow wedding bells,
    Golden bells!
    What a world of happiness their harmony foretells!

Bunched R

Round your lips slightly. Draw your tongue away from the front teeth. Press the sides of the back of your tongue against the upper molars. Hollow out the front of your tongue to make a bowl, but do not curl the tip backwards. Most importantly, the tip of the tongue should not touch anything! Make a continuing sound. Do not make an unnecessary vowel sound before your /r/. Your tongue position will change slightly with each following vowel:

Practice: Bunched R

reef	rot	bereave	merry
rip	raw	a rip	a raw one
rate	wrote	array	tomorrow
red	rude	very	fury
rabbit	rug	sorry	already

In the blend, release a stop before an /r/ at the same time as you begin the /r/. Make other sounds flow into the /r/ in clusters.

bring	preen	cream	green	three	spray
bread	pretty	cram	gray	though	spread
brash	pray	crumb	grab	free	sprawl
brought	product	crude	grub	fruit	scream
broke	prove	cry	grow	fry	scratch
brown	pride	crowd	grew	shrimp	scroll

In the case of /tr-/ and /dr-/, these are actually like single sounds. They are retroflexed; the tongue tip turns backwards and makes contact with the roof of the mouth. The /tr-/ should be quite aspirated.

tree	dream	street
tray	drip	string
trap	drop	straight
trot	drove	strew
true	draw	straw

Minimal pairs with /l, r/ contrasted:

reef → leaf	rock → lock
rip → lip	raw → law
raise → laze	rode → load

Minimal pairs in clusters:

pray → play	cray → clay
brew → blue	grow → glow
grad → glad	brush → blush
prop → plop	creek → clique
such → sir→ Certs	
gull → grrr → girl	
won → were → work → world	

Practice: Contrast /L/ and /R/

Use the following exercises. Form pairs. One person asks the question or makes the statement. The other person gives the corresponding reply.

Did he finish the rake?
> Yes, it's repaired; we can get the leaves up now.

Did he finish the lake?
> Yes, it will fill up when it rains again.

I cut the limb.
> Good. It was hanging too low.

I cut the rim.
> Oh, no! How will we get the tire back on?

I bought a new rug.
> Oh? What color is it?

I bought a new lug.
> Why just one? You need six to fix a tire.

Did you examine the new Reece agreement?
> Has Reece finished it yet?

Did you examine the new lease agreement?
> Yeah. It's for six months.

Vowel Chart With IPA Symbols

The IPA (International Phonetic Alphabet) symbols are beside the key words.

<table>
<tr><td colspan="3" align="center">Vowel Chart
The IPA (International Phonetic Alphabet) symbols
for the vowels are beside the key words.</td></tr>
<tr><td>Long Vowel Sounds</td><td>Short Vowel Sounds</td><td>Difficult Vowel Sounds</td></tr>
<tr><td>a   /ā/   face</td><td>a   /â/   apple</td><td>u: moon</td></tr>
<tr><td>e   /ē/   key</td><td>e   /ê/   egg</td><td>aw: b<u>all</u></td></tr>
<tr><td>i   /ī/   mice</td><td>I   /î/   in</td><td>a: car</td></tr>
<tr><td>o   /ō/   coat</td><td>o   /ô/   olive</td><td>ʊ   book</td></tr>
<tr><td>u   /ū/   music</td><td>u   /û/   up, cup</td><td>kaʊ   cow</td></tr>
<tr><td></td><td></td><td>bɔɪ   boy</td></tr>
<tr><td></td><td></td><td>ɝ   bird</td></tr>
<tr><td colspan="3" align="center">The schwa (ə) can replace any vowel in an unstressed position</td></tr>
</table>

BIBLIOGRAPHY

Celce-Murcia, Marianne, Donna M. Brinton, and Janet Goodwin. *Teaching Pronunciation, A Reference for TESOL.* Cambridge University Press. 1996.

Gilbert, Judy. *Clear Speech. ISBN 521-42118-7 Student.*

Schoenbach, et.al. *Reading for Understanding.* San Francisco. Jossey Bass Co.1999.

Snow, Don. *More Than A Native Speaker.* TESOL. Washington, DC. 1996.

Stevick, Earl W. *Memory Meaning and Method.* Newbury House, 1976

Woods, Howard B. *Rhythm and Stress.* About 1972. (Out of print, I think.)

Wong, Linda. *Essential Study Skills, Third Edition.* Boston. Houghton Mifflin. 2000.

Weinstein, Nina. *Whaddayasay?* Guided Practice in Relaxed English. 2nd ed. Prentice Hall Regents. ISBN0-201-670-40-2

ABOUT THE AUTHOR

Glenda Reece has been a teacher, a teacher trainer, an author, and a content creator for ESL and Cross Culture programs across the United States and in several foreign countries. She has trained foreign speaking ESL students and teachers in USA, China and South America. Her work has ranged from the North Carolina Governor's committee for refugee resettlement to high school ESL teacher to business owner and Literacy volunteer.

She has taught or led seminars for the Immigration and Refugee Center, the National Association of Foreign Student Advisors (NAFSA), Teachers of English to Speakers of Other Languages (TESOL), Southeastern Seminary, North Carolina State University, the University of North Carolina, Duke University, Wake County School System, and at Literacy Conferences in numerous states.

Glenda is the owner of ESL Training Services, which provides English and Cross Cultural training to international business professionals in the Raleigh, NC, area. She was an early president of the North and South Carolina chapter of TESOL. She has been recognized by the Baptist State Convention of North Carolina as Literacy Volunteer of the Year, and was presented the Mildred Blankenship National Volunteer of the Year Award by the North American Mission Board of the Southern Baptist Convention.

Glenda has taught individuals from all over the globe. Teaching is her first love, and her students are always the center to the session, whether it is one on one or a group of fifty.

She is the author of *Twelve Topics for ESL Beginners*, *Bible Verse Chants*, and *English Lessons from the Bible: The Book of Mark*.

Glenda has produced several training videos including *Conversational English Using the Lipson Method*, *The Oral Interview Procedure*, and *Getting Serious About Top-Down and Bottom-Up Pronunciation*.

www.ingramcontent.com/pod-product-compliance
Lightning Source LLC
Chambersburg PA
CBHW081631040426
42449CB00014B/3265